The Deadly Sins of Employee Retention

NEW EDITION TO SOLVE THE GREAT RESIGNATION, QUIET QUITTING, BURNOUT, AND MORE

Table of Contents

Introduction

Deadly Sin #1   Treating Everyone Equally

Deadly Sin #2   One Size Fits All

Deadly Sin #3   Not Listening Deeply

Deadly Sin #4   Overcomplicating Your Solutions

Deadly Sin #5   Neglecting The First 90 Days

Deadly Sin #6   Letting Them Leave

Deadly Sin #7   Turning Your Back

Conclusion

Introduction

IN THE FALL OF 2022, as we write this new edition, nearly half of employees are looking for other jobs. Employees are quitting their jobs far more frequently than before the pandemic. There are currently more than ten million open jobs.

The word "unprecedented" is overused in business books, but we can probably all agree that this time, it's justified. The likes of the Great Resignation haven't been experienced in our lifetimes; the pandemic and the attendant human and economic costs, working from home, the strain on essential workers, turnover and burnout at historic levels, and the list goes on.

And beyond the record numbers of overt resignations, we've now also got the phenomenon known as Quiet Quitting. It's a mentality that advocates remaining employed while performing the job's requirements and nothing more. For a decent percentage of workers, Quiet Quitting is the understandable and predictable result of some companies exploiting employees' willingness to go above and beyond, stay late, etc., without reward or recognition. Of course, there are situations where some difficult personalities use Quiet Quitting as an excuse for disengaging or even coasting. But either way, with the stress and burnout facing today's employees, it's unrealistic to think that working life would return to its pre-pandemic state. The bottom line is that the need to retain (and inspire) employees has been quickly elevated from an important activity to an urgent, four-alarm fire, with all hands on deck.

Yet, notwithstanding the desperate need for employee retention, most organizations and their leaders are making serious mistakes. We've studied more than 1,000,000 leaders, and we've identified the Deadly Sins of Employee Retention. These are the 7 mistakes that can destroy an organization's retention efforts. The bad news is that they're so harmful. The good news is that they're easily corrected.

This book will challenge some of the most entrenched and misguided beliefs about employee retention. We'll show you how to avoid the Deadly Sins of Employee Retention and teach you seven elegantly simple strategies for keeping your best people.

In this book, we're not going to recommend grandiose gestures. You don't have to rewrite all your HR policies or spend seven figures on outside consultants. We're going to point out 7 simple mistakes that most leaders and organizations make, and we're going to give you instantly-actionable techniques for correcting them.

The techniques aren't complicated. If you avoid the Deadly Sins of Employee Retention, you will achieve benchmark results. And if you get your colleagues onboard, your whole organization will be transformed.

DEADLY SIN #1
Treating Everyone Equally

THE GREAT RESIGNATION (OR THE Great Attrition, or the Great Renegotiation, or whatever name you choose) is real. As we write this new edition in the latter half of 2022, voluntary quit rates are more than 25% higher than pre-pandemic levels, and there are 10+ million open jobs. We could go on with dozens of statistics about the size of the current problem, but all those statistics share a common flaw.

Imagine you're the Director of the Emergency Room at a large downtown hospital. It's a Saturday night, and the evening shift is just coming on. You're expecting tonight to be busy because it's a full moon, and it's always crazy on a full moon. All of a sudden, the receptionist runs into our office and tells you that Pat, one of your nurses, just called in and quit. But you employ two nurses named Pat, both of whom are scheduled to work tonight. One of them is a brilliant nurse, respected by staff, doctors, and patients. The other Pat is mediocre at best and a real thorn in your side most of the time. Which of these nurses' departures will hurt you (and which one might actually help you)?

Imagine you run a 5-star restaurant. It's a Friday afternoon, you're several hours from opening for dinner, and tonight the restaurant is fully booked. While you're sitting in your office, your assistant rushes in and tells you that there's a nasty message on the voicemail from Bob, quitting his job and vowing never to set foot in your restaurant again. The problem is that you employ two guys named Bob, both of whom are scheduled to work tonight. One Bob is your head chef, and the other is a busser. Which of these Bob's departures could irreparably damage your restaurant?

The Declaration of Independence tells us that everyone is created equal. From a moral and political perspective, we couldn't agree more. But from an organizational perspective, just because we were all created equal doesn't mean we end up that way. In the eyes of customers, some individuals are more important than others, and some job categories are more important than others. And some individuals and job categories can more directly and significantly impact your organization's success (or failure).

STOP CALCULATING TURNOVER

Have you ever seen a soap opera with twins? They're always played by the same actor, so they look exactly alike on the surface. But when you peel back that perfectly coifed veneer, one twin is always good, and the other is always evil (and usually trying to kill the good twin). If a soap opera can have a moral, twins could represent the lesson that "appearances can be deceiving."

Why the digression into soap operas? Because turnover statistics are the soap opera twins of the business world.

Imagine you're about to have major surgery, and you have a choice of hospitals: AnyTown Hospital or MyTown Medical Center. Both have new facilities, TV ads that tug at your heartstrings, and exactly the same annual turnover rates – 16 percent. They're so outwardly indistinguishable that if this were all the information you had available, you'd have to flip a coin to choose between them.

But let's pretend that you do a little investigating, and you find that while these hospitals look the same on the outside, they're very different inside. While they have the same overall turnover, AnyTown Hospital's turnover is heaviest in roles like housekeepers, kitchen staff, and financial office personnel (while very few nurses and pharmacists leave). But at MyTown Medical Center, turnover is heaviest in nursing and pharmacist roles (while housekeepers and kitchen staff rarely leave).

Have you discovered the evil twin? Both hospitals look the same (16% turnover), but one of these hospitals is much more likely to kill you (MyTown

Medical Center). Turnover numbers, as they're typically calculated, don't tell you much.

Even if we knew which job roles were suffering the highest turnover, we'd still be missing information about whether we were losing high performers or low performers.

Imagine you're a stock analyst for a Wall Street research firm, and your job is to determine whether certain companies are doing well or about to fail. You've been researching a large software company (we'll call them Mircospot). You just got a tip that 400 programmers have abruptly left the company. Before you can write your analysis about how the loss of these 400 programmers will impact Mircospot, you should probably ask a few questions. Any ideas? Here's a question we'd like to ask: *Were these 400 programmers high performers or low performers?*

As the saying goes: There are lies, damn lies, and statistics. Before you get too fixated on a number, make sure it's telling you what you think it's telling you.

Some People Are More Important Than Others

When Michael Jordan played for the Chicago Bulls, an assistant coach caught Michael after practice and chastised him for being too selfish. "Michael," he said, "there's no I in TEAM." Michael stopped, looked at the coach quizzically and replied, "No, but there is in WIN."

Some individuals are more important than others, and some job categories are more important than others. Let's start with individuals.

Individuals

Do you have an employee you'd like to clone? A high performer who's always early, anticipates your every request, is dependable, unflappable, handles pressure, stays late, and delivers exceptional service to your customers? Someone who closes deals, saves lives, fixes and prevents problems, and provides informal leadership to other employees?

Do you also know their evil twin? A low performer who's chronically late, complains constantly, resists change, questions every directive, and isn't very good at their job? Someone who traumatizes customers, destroys productivity and morale, and makes leaders' lives more difficult?

When you go to your favorite restaurant, are you hoping for the chef who lives to create culinary masterpieces or the chef who frequently scratches himself and believes in the 5-second rule? When you go to the bank, are you hoping for the teller who's efficient and cheerful or the teller who's as fast and friendly as a three-legged tortoise with a toothache?

High performers matter more than low performers. And every study, ours included, indicates that the more an organization focuses on retaining high performers and eliminating low performers, the more successful that organization will be.

But here, we need to ring an alarm bell about what's happening to many high performers.

Given the importance of great employees, it's safe to assume that no executive sets out to create a company culture that's unappealing, let alone damaging, to high performers. And yet, as shocking as this sounds, that's what happens in far too many organizations.

In a recent Leadership IQ study, we discovered that nearly half of organizations had created a poor experience for their best people. If that wasn't bad enough, in those companies, low performers were actually happier. So the best people are potential flight risks, while the least effective ones are likely to stay.

By matching an employee's engagement survey scores with their annual performance appraisal data for 207 organizations, we learned that being a top-rated employee doesn't equal happiness or fulfillment. In fact, in 42% of the companies we studied, people with the highest performance appraisal scores had lower employee engagement than those with the lowest appraisal scores.

How is it possible that your mostly highly-rated employees could be less engaged than your people with the lowest appraisal scores? Well, think about what life's like for many high performers.

Imagine that you (the boss) have just been told that you've got to make a major presentation in 48 hours. And if you mess it up, your career will suffer. You're going to need one of your workers to pull an all-nighter and help you create this presentation. Who are you going to ask to suffer with you for the next two days — your best employee or your worst one?

Of course, you'll ask your best person.

When this same situation happens again a few weeks later, who will you task with pulling the all-nighter? Once again, you'll ask your best employee.

Play this out in your head a few more times and ask yourself, "When stuff hits the fan, or the pressure gets high, who do I ask to work their tails off and make things right?" What you'll typically find is that every department has one, two, or three people who consistently get tasked with the toughest projects, the tightest deadlines, and the most stressful situations. It's not because they're terrible and we want them to suffer; it's because they're the best. But in many companies, being a high performer means having the toughest job.

Making matters worse is that while your high performer goes without sleep for 48 hours to create an amazing slide deck for your big presentation, your worst employee had a relaxed dinner at home followed by a full night's sleep.

Perhaps you reward your high performers for their extraordinary effort with a little extra recognition or a bigger bonus. But sadly, that doesn't happen very often (and even when it does, it's typically inconsequential).

In another study, we found that 96% of employees, managers, and CEOs agree that high performers should receive more rewards and recognition than low performers. But only 22% said their leader always distinguishes between high and low performers, while 45% said their leader never or rarely does so.

Clearly, lots of companies struggle to differentiate and appropriately reward or recognize their best performers. Maybe this wouldn't be as problematic if those organizations were instead offering high performers amazing growth and development opportunities. Alas, in another of our studies, we discovered that only 20% of employees say that their leader always takes an active role in helping them grow and develop their full potential. By contrast, 29% of employees say that their leader never or rarely takes an active role in helping them grow.

Our high performers often work harder, volunteer more, and respond at all hours. That's great, and it's part of what makes them high performers. But the downside is that if we consistently work them into the ground without rest, reward or development, we risk them quitting.

JOB CATEGORIES

Retention isn't just about individuals, however. It's also about knowing which job categories are most critical to your survival. Customers may consider some job categories more important than others. Some labor markets are tighter than others. Some job categories are simply harder and more expensive to replace. Some jobs require years of education and on-the-job training before an individual can be considered competent. And for some jobs there is no formal education, just years of company-specific training and on-the-job apprenticeship.

Nurses, pharmacists, respiratory therapists, and radiologic technicians are in short supply in many regions. Skilled trades like plumbers, electricians, and welders can be tough to find. Current global shortages for engineers and programmers are forecasted to slow the growth of entire economies, let alone individual companies.

Then there are jobs like Crystal Cutter. These are the folks who create the intricate designs on the fancy crystal vases and champagne flutes displayed so beautifully (if idly) in your china cabinet. It can take 7-10 years to become a master cutter.

Or take the job of Enterprise Software Architect. One of our technology clients develops proprietary software applications for organizing responses to large-scale disasters (yes, it's a rapid-growth business). Even their most seasoned hires can require 6 months of on-the-job tutoring before they understand the ins and outs of their applications.

WHERE TO PUT YOUR RETENTION EFFORTS

Assuming you've got limited time and money with which to retain your most important people, where do you expend your resources? High performers are obviously more important to keep than low performers, and hard-to-replace jobs are more important than easy-to-replace jobs. But how do you reconcile these two issues?

Retention Priority Map

	Low	Medium	High
High Performer	Medium-Low Priority	Medium Priority	Top Priority
Middle Performer	Low Priority	Medium Priority	Top Priority
Low Performer	Low Priority	Low Priority	Low Priority

Costly, difficult, disruptive to replace

The Retention Priority map tells us where we should be putting our time, for the sake of the organization's success and our customers' loyalty. On the horizontal axis is the difficulty of replacing this role. Nurses, welders, and specialized software engineers might be costly, disruptive, and difficult to replace (and thus fall in the High category).

On the vertical axis is the level of performance for a particular individual. If we want to clone this person, they're a high performer. And if we're wondering what sins we committed in a past life to deserve this person, they're a low performer. (If they're somewhere in between, you've probably got a middle performer.)

One twist you'll notice is that a high performer in an easier-to-replace role can be a lesser priority than a middle performer in a tough-to-replace role. In a market where pharmacists are impossible to find, your average pharmacist is going to emerge as a higher retention priority than your superstar financial analyst (assuming financial analysts are easier to find).

The market has a lot to say about where we put our retention efforts. If the market says, "nurses are in very short supply," and you know that it's going to be costly, time-consuming, and highly disruptive to your patients if you lose a nurse, then you absolutely have to retain your nurses, even if they're just middle performers. But remember, no matter how scarce a role may be, if the individual in that role is a low performer, they're never a retention priority.

The key to retention is balancing the need for high performers in every role and the demands of often volatile labor markets. Follow the Retention Priority Map, and you'll know where to focus your retention efforts.

THE EVOLUTION OF A CLASSIC EXAMPLE

In the first edition of this book, we described a classic example of how to use the Retention Priority Map. We anonymized the name of the company, somewhat, calling them BrownEx; a well-known package delivery company with big trucks rushing around town delivering packages within a guaranteed delivery time. Here's the example we presented:

At BrownEx, one of their top priority jobs is the Delivery Driver. Drivers are the frontline of customer service and maintain the closest customer relationships. Drivers also drive BrownEx's profitability (and thus their profits). While the company employs advanced route-mapping software to guide drivers from one delivery to another, anyone who's ever used a mapping app on their phone knows that there's the "by the book" route, and then there's the best (and fastest) route. The fastest routes are idiosyncratic and usually involve alleys, side streets, avoiding certain intersections, etc. Not only are the routes idiosyncratic, but the customers are as well. Some customers are always late; some are always early; some always have heavy packages; some just send overnight envelopes, etc.

The bottom line is that it can take months for a driver to learn the idiosyncrasies of the routes and the customers. So losing a driver is incredibly disruptive to the organization.

But losing drivers is just what was happening. BrownEx had high turnover in the driver job and, worse, was losing high and middle performers. So they started analyzing the situation (using techniques you'll learn in the next few chapters) and discovered that a major source of driver flight was loading the trucks. It turns out that not only did drivers have to deliver the packages, but they also had to load the trucks before their routes started. Imagine being a driver in Dallas in the summer, loading trucks in 100-degree heat in a thick, dark uniform and then sticking to a vinyl seat for an hour as you enter the parking lot known as rush hour.

The obvious solution was simply to eliminate the loading activities from the driver's job and give them to somebody else. But would anyone take the loading activities?

It's hot, sweaty, back-breaking work, and whoever does that work is not going to stay with the company very long.

Turns out none of that matters. The loading work is inexpensive, easy to learn (30 minutes vs. several months), and doesn't require any special degrees or licenses. And you can employ students, part-timers, or basically anyone with a pulse who can lift 50 pounds. In short, if this role has high turnover, it doesn't matter.

BrownEx created this new Loader role, and as soon as they did, driver turnover went down. In fact, they cut driver turnover by 50% in under 6 months. Sure, the turnover for loaders is about 200%, but they're so easy to replace and train, it doesn't matter. BrownEx kept their most valuable people (customers love them and the company needs them), and that's what makes them successful.

The solution they devised, dividing a role into higher and lower retention priorities, is as sound now as it was then. But as the world continues to change, you'll have to keep refining and adapting your retention strategies.

July of 2022 was the sixth-hottest July in the 143-year global climate record. And according to a recent article in the Guardian, "In early July, 2022 in California, UPS driver Esteban Chavez, 24, collapsed and died while working as temperatures rose to the high 90s. A video from a Ring surveillance camera also went viral in July showing a UPS driver collapsing on a porch in excessive heat."

The UPS trucks generally do not have air conditioning. Drivers have reported temperatures in the back of their trucks near or at 130 degrees Fahrenheit. The Teamsters Union, which represents 350,000 UPS workers, has given UPS a two-week notice to provide detailed information on any plan the company has to protect employees, combat heat illness, and install or replace relief equipment for workers.

At the time of publication, we don't know exactly how this will end. But we do know that while the original example (creating the Loader role to relieve stress on Drivers) worked wonderfully, increasing temperatures require additional new strategies. The lesson for every company is that your employee retention strategies will always have to adjust to market conditions and to the makeup of your workforce.

The bottom line is that some individuals and some job categories are more important than others. Your first task is to figure out who's who and retain the people that keep you in business.

DEADLY SIN #2
One Size Fits All

PAUL, CHRISTINE, BILL, AND SUE are all financial analysts at StayHealthy Inc., a large Midwestern insurance company. They're all around 40 years old, they all have kids, they all drink coffee, they're all married, they've all tried Atkins and South Beach diets, and they all went to college and graduate school. In short, these folks are pretty demographically similar. But that doesn't mean they're motivated by the same things.

Paul is driven by money. Not by ostentatious displays of wealth but by having financial security (i.e., money in the bank). He doesn't care about the particulars of his job; within reason, he'd do whatever job pays him the most money. When StayHealthy's new pay-for-performance plan went into effect, his job performance shot right up. The bigger the bonus, the harder he works. Of course, without that plan or a comparable way to increase his income, he'd likely be out the door tomorrow.

Christine is easily bored. She's an adrenaline junkie and needs to do interesting and cutting-edge work. If there's a new or experimental project, she's all over it. Also, she doesn't suffer fools gladly and thus often works by herself. Give her a risky project with lots of autonomy, and she's ecstatic. Put her with a large group of mediocre minds doing boring work, and she's ready to take a header off her cubical wall.

Bill is driven by a need to feel good about himself and the work he does. Ever since the birth of his daughter, he's been gripped by a sense of existential inadequacy. He's concerned with making the world a better place and showing his little princess that he makes a difference. Last month he worked on a project that developed creative ways to offer health insurance to very poor families, and he was more driven and productive than he's ever been.

Sue needs control. She's emotionally attached to her work area and her work product. And she is not a fan of people messing with "her area." She's territorial but very competent.

When she's in control, she's highly motivated. If she lost that control, she'd lose her desire to work for StayHealthy Inc.

Imagine that you manage Paul, Christine, Bill, and Sue. How do you retain them? Is an organization-wide, or even a department-wide, strategy going to work? How about a new pay-for-performance plan, flexible work schedules, or an organization-wide raise?

Is there any one cure-all approach that will work?

THE FALLACY OF THE "AVERAGE PERSON"

Both of the authors were raised in Buffalo, NY. While we eventually moved further south to escape the intense winters, we remain die-hard fans of the Buffalo Bills. So we're going to use a sports example to make a point. The average NFL player weighs 245 pounds and is 6'1 ½" tall. (*We knew NFL players were pretty big guys, so nothing shocking here.*) But what's fascinating is that there is not one single player on the Buffalo Bills who either weighs 245 pounds or is 6'1 ½" tall. And, of course, there are no players who match both averages (i.e., weighs 245 pounds and is 6'1 ½" tall).

One day we assigned one of our researchers to scour the rosters of every NFL team, looking for the average player (who weighs 245 pounds and is 6'1 ½" tall). It was pretty tedious work, so we let him stop after 10 teams, but he was unable to find even one player that matched the NFL average.

What's the point of this exercise? Averages lie. Averages are misleading. Nobody is "average," and if you go looking for the "average" person, you will probably never find them. (Have you ever seen a family with 2.5 kids?)

This same "Fallacy of the Average Person" holds true when we're talking about employee retention. Some people quit their organization because they don't like their hours. Some desire more flexibility. Some want better benefits, while others want more cash in their pockets. Some can't stand their boss; others dislike their coworkers. Some want career advancement; others want to do their current job without being pushed to climb any higher. Like the StayHealthy, Inc. folks in our opening example, everyone is driven by something a little different.

We've asked more than 100,000 employees to describe why they choose to stay at a company. As you might expect, the answers are all over the place. Some people say it's interesting and challenging work, while others say career advancement opportunities. For some, it's whether the company is well managed, whether they have a good relationship with their boss, or they feel in sync with the company's values. There are those who stay because the company recognizes and rewards high performers, others remain because the compensation is good, and for some it's because the job fits their schedule. In short, there is no single answer why people stay in their jobs.

If you look at exit interview studies, you find similar results. In organization-wide studies, people usually say they quit for reasons that include lack of recognition or rewards; lack of advancement opportunities; lack of feedback from management; not being made to feel like a valued employee; lack of training and education; uncompetitive compensation; and lack of responsibility.

If you can distill these responses into one universal reason people stay or quit an organization, you deserve a medal. We've tried, and it just doesn't work.

We hope we've made the point that people are unique and tend to be motivated by different things. But most organizations still haven't gotten the message. Every day we see companies implement organization-wide strategies that utilize a limited number of techniques to retain the entire workforce (desperately hoping to find that "average" employee).

The problem goes beyond the fact that this is an amazingly inefficient way to retain people. While these organizations institute the new systems, they're ignoring the needs of everyone else. If 20% of the workforce is going to be retained because the organization instituted this new system (and that's being very generous), what happens to the other 80% that got missed? What about their retention needs? Are we willing to let these people walk out the door?

As if this weren't enough, there's one more complicating factor we have to address. There are a decent number of cases where people just don't know why they stay or leave. The things that drive them in or out of an organization operate on a subconscious level.

Let's take a classic case in which we have a highly-gifted programmer who gets promoted to manager. It turns out that this programmer-turned-manager is a terrible manager. (As we all know, the best programmer, the best nurse, the best engineer, or the best welder does not always make the best manager.) This guy is terrible at being a manager, and he's deeply unhappy. But he doesn't realize that it's the new job that's making him unhappy. So he now begins to think it's the company that's making him unhappy, and he quits. He joins another company, but this time he joins as a manager, not as a programmer. The cycle of unhappiness starts all over again, and he quits this new job as well. And on and on the cycle goes.

This whole section leads up to our argument for radically changing how we retain our employees. We had to be thorough here because, notwithstanding all this evidence, most managers refuse to accept that every individual is unique. Many managers have difficulty grasping the idea that every individual stays and quits for very different reasons.

A whopping 89% of managers believe that money is the biggest reason why employees quit. We've asked thousands of managers, "Why did your employees quit?" and overwhelmingly, they say, "My employees quit because somebody else offered them more money." Of course, as you can guess from the previous pages, most employees don't quit because of the money. Some do, especially in a company that egregiously underpays its employees, but, overall, 91% of employees say money had nothing to do with their decision to leave.

ONE SIZE FITS ONE

We hope we've made it clear that there is not a universal, magical, silver-bullet, cure-all retention tactic that works for every employee. If there was, we wouldn't need this book. Instead, we'd write a book called *The Magic Answer to Retention: Do This One Thing And Everybody Stays*. And it'd be about 10 pages long and sell for a million dollars.

The only retention approach that can succeed is to engage each employee 1:1. If we want to figure out why people stay and/or leave, we're going to have to ask them. The greatest organizations, the ones who do the best job of retaining their top people, spend the most time engaging 1:1 with their employees.

When we talk about engaging employees 1:1, what we're really talking about is a conversation between the manager and an individual employee to diagnose what drives them (what keeps them here and what could make them quit).

Of course, if we're talking about folks that we'd love to see quit the organization (e.g., Talented Terrors), then we're not going to worry too much about having these quarterly conversations. But for the folks we want to keep (our top and medium priorities as identified in the previous chapter), we need quarterly conversations at a minimum. The best organizations, and the best leaders, conduct these conversations at least once a month. If you start with every quarter, however, you'll still be far ahead of your competitors.

Finally, these are mandatory conversations. If retaining your most important employees is an organizational priority, these conversations must be a managerial priority. Later in the chapter, we'll show you how to institute these conversations as a mandatory procedure, but for now, it's sufficient to say that every leader must commit to these conversations, from the CEO on down.

SHOVES AND TUGS

Here is one of the most important lessons about engaging your employees: everyone has Shoves and Tugs. Shoves are issues that demotivate you, drain your energy, stop you from putting forth maximum effort, and make you want to quit; they "shove" you out the door. Tugs are factors that motivate and fulfill you, make you want to deliver maximum effort, and keep you coming back every day; they "tug" at you to stay.

This seems simple enough, but here's the twist: Shoves and Tugs aren't flip sides of the same coin. Just because somebody has multiple Tugs during a week doesn't mean they don't have any Shoves. So, before you start trying to figure out how to provide people with meaningful Tugs, you've got to at least acknowledge, and ideally mitigate, their Shoves. If you don't, and those Shoves remain unaddressed, then employee engagement will take a dive, and people will quit.

Let me begin with an analogy that's unconventional but that might help clarify this issue. Just as Shoves and Tugs are not opposites, neither are pain and pleasure. The opposite of pleasure isn't pain; it's just the absence of pleasure. Similarly, the opposite of pain isn't pleasure; it's just the absence of pain. If somebody is hitting my foot with a hammer, that's pain. When the hammering stops, it's not pleasure; there is just no more pain. If I'm getting the world's greatest back rub, that's pleasure. When it stops, it's not pain; it is simply no more pleasure.

Here's the lesson: If I'm getting a great back rub, it does not preclude someone from simultaneously hitting my foot with a hammer. If that happens, then the pain in my foot will totally detract from the pleasure I'm getting from the back rub. Here's a corollary lesson: If you walk past me one day and see that my foot is being hit with a hammer, then you cannot fix the pain in my foot by giving me a back rub. The only way to stop the pain in my foot is to stop the hammer from hitting it. And unfortunately, discovering those hammers has not typically been a goal for most leaders.

Every day, in organizations around the world, employees' feet are being hit with hammers and their bosses' solution isn't to stop the hammer (i.e., eliminate the Shove), but rather to offer a back rub (i.e., offer a Tug). It's a big reason why so many employees are looking to leave their current jobs, and less than a third of employees are highly engaged.

Consider, for example, a software development team in Silicon Valley led by a manager named Chris. The department was on a heavy deadline to finish a new product, and Chris' mounting anxiety was causing him to micromanage. He began instituting numerous "check-in" meetings, widely acknowledged by the team as useless, and insisting on regular "no-work team lunch hours" that forced employees to work extra hours in order to stay on track to make the deadline.

Chris could feel the high emotional tension throughout the department, but rather than asking his team about the source of their frustration, he decided to take the team to Catalina Island for the weekend to relax. He figured it was a great way to offer a nice reward and get everyone's brains back into the game. When he made the announcement, more than a few of the programmers' heads nearly exploded. The last thing they wanted was more time with one another, just hanging out and not working. They wanted to finish the project, hit the deadline, and go home to their families. They wanted to stop wasting time at work and just get the job done.

Chris made the mistake of trying to fix a Shove with a Tug, and it backfired. Yes, Catalina Island is beautiful, and perhaps in another circumstance, it would have been a nice reward and a way to boost employee engagement. But with his team already feeling the Shove of spending too much time away from the actual work of programming, not only was the Tug a poor choice, but Chris' credibility took a big blow by his insensitive lack of understanding as to what was really demoralizing his team.

When good employees must function in a Shove environment, such as dealing with low performers, stubborn roadblocks, or a terrible working environment, it's akin to being hit on the foot with a hammer multiple times. When you're suffering that level of pain, Tugs, such as autonomy (the power to control an entire process and the ability to work on innovative projects with great teams) aren't going to have a positive impact until you remove or reduce the frequency and severity of the Shoves.

The big lesson is that if you desire to improve employee engagement, then introducing Tugs alone will not work. Take the time to discover, acknowledge and, if possible, eliminate the Shoves.

A Shoves and Tugs conversation doesn't have to be formal; in fact, it's actually better if it is not. The last thing you want is to make it seem like a performance appraisal. Get out from behind your desk and invite employees to have a casual conversation over coffee or lunch, anywhere two people can have a reasonably private conversation for 10-20 minutes.

If your employees are remote, don't make a phone call (or, gasp, send an email). Use applications like Skype or Facetime, both of which you can utilize right from your phone. These are simple ways to get something approximating face-to-face conversations, with tone of voice, two-way interactivity, and some level of body language. This allows you to express yourself more fully and to get the visual and physical feedback needed from others to hold authentic and meaningful conversations. Virtually all mobile devices now include front-facing cameras, making video calling easy to use and highly accessible.

This conversation should take place at least once every quarter, although once a month is even better. In the majority of cases, these two simple questions are all you need to ask:

- SHOVES QUESTION: "Could you tell me about a time in the past month or two when you felt demotivated (or

frustrated, or emotionally burnt out)?"
- TUGS QUESTION: "Could you tell me about a time in the past month or two when you felt motivated (or excited, or jazzed up)?"

Use language that feels natural for you, and bear in mind that you're not asking these questions simply for the sake of asking questions; you actually want to know the answers. You'll typically find that the issues raised by these questions are as different as people's hair color or their choice of ties. Each person is a little bit different, so find out exactly what motivates and demotivates each individual.

It's natural to wonder if asking these questions will make employees think twice about the demotivators that they face. Could you be putting negative ideas into their heads? My response is that just because you have an EKG at a checkup, it doesn't mean that you're more likely to have a heart attack. If you are screened for breast or prostate cancer, it doesn't mean that you're more likely to develop those cancers. If you're at risk of a heart attack, getting a good cardiac workup will uncover that hidden risk. It may be scary to learn that your risk is high, and that is why so many don't get the necessary tests —but the tests don't cause the illness. The real question is, do you want to bury your head in the sand, or do you want a team of followers who are happy at work?

ASKING FOR BOTH SHOVES AND TUGS

Asking about both motivators and demotivators tends to be a radical concept for most leaders, so let's walk through another example.

Pat is a nursing researcher at a major teaching hospital. She's worked there for 8 years and thinks it's a great place to work. She loves doing research, and this organization has hundreds of ongoing studies on which she can participate and even publish. Her major Tug is doing intellectually challenging work with really smart people. But two weeks ago, the hospital instituted new work schedules, and they changed all the shifts. This is causing Pat serious difficulty because she had timed her kids' schedules around her old shift start/end times, and now this disrupts everything. For Pat, this scheduling change is a Shove.

If we had only asked Pat what excited her about her job, what really made her love this hospital, we'd have gotten an answer about doing intellectually stimulating work. And if we had only asked Pat what could make her life sufficiently miserable to cause her resignation, we'd have gotten an answer about her schedule and her outside-of-work obligations. It's only when we ask about both issues that we get the complete picture.

When you're working with low performers, when you're working terrible hours, or you've got a terrible working environment, you could be so frustrated that you feel like you're being Shoved out the door. You could feel so frustrated that you no longer notice all of the other good things about your job that Tug at you to stay – the autonomy, the ability to have control over an entire process, the ability to work on innovative projects and teams. If you're like the organizations in our studies, more than a third of your workforce could feel this way. And these people are huge retention risks.

On the other hand, you could have a working environment free from Shoves, but also lacking any significant Tugs. You're not being Shoved out the door by frustration, but neither are you being Tugged to remain at the company. If you're like the organizations in our studies, as much as half of your workforce could feel this way. The good news is that these people probably aren't spending their days on Indeed or CareerBuilder actively applying for jobs. The bad news is that if the economy changes, or one of your competitors makes a play for them, or they just happen across another opportunity, they will leave.

To get someone really truly committed to your organization, you must eliminate any Shoves and fulfill at least some of their Tugs. In essence, you've got to meet their basic needs and afford some opportunity to address their high-order needs.

Discovering Shoves May Be Scary, But It's Necessary

Every company is scrambling to retain its best employees, and that's no easy feat given that burnout numbers are still terrible and engagement scores are low. That's why so many companies are experimenting with everything from retention bonuses, greater work-from-home flexibility, and hiring bonuses to backfill the employees that have quit. But all those techniques and motivators are unlikely to work if companies don't first acknowledge a painful reality.

Before a company can retain its employees, it first has to stop frustrating and demotivating them (i.e., remove the Shoves).

In the study, Frustration At Work, Leadership IQ surveyed 2,553 employees to assess the biggest frustrations and roadblocks that were keeping them from being as productive as they could be. Among the major discoveries was that around 60% of employees say their frustrations at work are so severe that they want to look for other jobs, and 84% said that fixing their frustrations would make them significantly more productive.

While workload and staffing comprised the top two categories of frustrations, about 39% combined, the remaining frustrations were spread across issues like toxic coworkers, insufficient or poor management, and a lack of clear direction. In other words, while a lack of staff and increasing workloads get most of the press, there are myriad other frustrations that make employees want to quit.

Imagine that you're an employee who regularly gives maximum effort at work; you clean up the messes left by less-effective coworkers, your customer service goes above and beyond, and you live the company's values without exception. Now imagine that, whether from inattention or lack of courage, your manager fails to recognize you for going above and beyond everyone else. Or imagine that your manager lets your coworkers get away with not living the company's values even though you exert extra effort to exemplify those values.

How frustrated would you be? Frustrated enough to quit? And would a small retention bonus or an extra week of vacation be enough to offset this pain? Even if you're not frustrated enough to overtly quit, would you be demotivated enough to ponder Quiet Quitting? Faced with situations like this, most people would seriously consider dialing back their efforts. If you're regularly going above and beyond without recognition, or worse, having even more work dumped on your desk, wouldn't you become a bit disillusioned?

The research is pretty clear that frustrations (aka Shoves) that severe, have to be addressed directly.

Don't Ask "How's It Going?"

More than a few managers think that they're asking about Shoves and Tugs when, in reality, all they're doing is asking employees something like, "How's it going?"

"How's it going?" is a question that managers ask employees all the time, and there are many similar versions of it in most other languages and cultures. It seems harmless enough, but asking "How's it going?" is actually one of the worst things you can ask employees if you really want deep insight. Linguists call it a phatic expression or a speech act; it's small talk, a conversation ritual that doesn't seek or offer any information of value. It's aimless social intercourse, and it's not even a real question. The purpose of a question is to elicit information, but the standard response most people give when asked "How's it going?" is "Everything's fine." There's no information gleaned, we just sit there and nod our heads when we get the expected response, but nothing is actually being said.

We don't typically ask "How's it going?" with the expectation that the other person will give a detailed account of what's happening in their life. Just like saying "Nice weather we're having" or "How about those Mets!" (both also phatic expressions), "How's it going" is lazy communication. And most people know that, which is why they usually respond "Everything's fine," and leave it at that. Phatic communication doesn't extend an invitation to have a real conversation. Every now and then, there will be an exception, like our neighbor who constantly violates the conversation ritual of "How's it going?" Instead of giving the expected reply of "Everything's fine," he launches into a detailed report on his bad hip, his troubled marriage, his needy kids, and his lemon of a car. But most people just say, "Everything's fine." And if "Everything's fine" is what you're hearing from your employees, it's trouble.

Assess Your Conversations

How your people answer your Shoves and Tugs questions will provide clues so you can assess how the conversation is progressing and if you need to push for more information.

There are four levels to look for:

The Superficial Level: This is when the employee answers, "Everything is fine. I can't think of anything." This person is actively avoiding the issue. We all can point to a time in the past 90 days when something either pleased us or ticked us off.

The Suspicious Level: If you hear a response that sounds like, "I'm sure there are things, but why do you want to know?" it shows the employee is acknowledging awareness of issues but fears that revealing those issues might result in trouble or even getting fired.

The Involved Level: If the employee tells you about a specific problem but offers no recommended solution, there's clear evidence of a Shove. But there is still a level of distrust. Build trust by providing more evidence of how far you are willing to go to fix the situation.

The Committed Level: If the employee gives you a full-blown description of a Shove, even if it pertains to you, and tells you specifically what should be done to fix it, you've hit the Shoves and Tugs jackpot.

If you find yourself stuck at the superficial level, it's probably an indication that you don't have a great history with this person. You might get the employee to loosen up a bit if you change the focus to a third-person approach. It's always safer to talk about your own stuff when you pretend it belongs to someone else.

To make the shift into third-person, ask a question such as: "What are the two to three things you think other employees like best about this organization?" Or you can ask, "Can you imagine reasons why employees would leave this company?"

When you're really stuck, and neither the primary nor the third-person questions are working, here are some other Shoves and Tugs questions you can try:

- Do you know any employees who have left?
- Do you know why they left?

- What are the 2-3 things you think other employees like least about this organization?
- Can you imagine reasons why employees would leave this company?
- If somebody asked you about the single worst part of working here, what would it be?
- What are the 2-3 things you think other employees like best about this organization?
- What are the 2-3 things you like best about this organization?
- Why do you think employees stay at this company?
- If you had to tell somebody about the single best part of working here, what would it be?

What should you do when you're not getting enough deep answers from your team, when you're hearing too many superficial and suspicious responses? If you talk to 10 employees and only one person tells you a Shove—perhaps the person reports a distaste for being micromanaged, especially on repetitive tasks—you've got something to work with. Let everyone witness your efforts to rein in your tendencies to micromanage. The news of "Wow, she didn't fire me! She actually did what I asked!" will spread fast. The following month, when you have your next set of Shoves and Tugs talks, you'll get a few more employees who will feel safe speaking up. Eventually, you'll gain most people's trust.

It takes courage for employees to tell the boss tough things such as, "Well, sometimes you micromanage me, and it really turns me off." And the fact may be that the person describing this Shove needs to be micromanaged from time to time. However, if you come back with a comment like, "Well, if you didn't screw up so much, I wouldn't have to micromanage you," you'll shut down any chance of productive communication. It takes practice to hold your tongue, but a Shoves and Tugs conversation isn't about how you feel or why you (or the organization) act the way you do. For that moment, it's all about the other person. So get used to calmly nodding your head and saying, "I hear you." [Note: In the next chapter, we'll give you techniques for greatly enhancing your listening skills for these conversations].

There will be Shoves that are outside your control and that you simply can't fix. But don't jump to this conclusion just because you don't see an immediate or obvious way out. Listen to what your employees tell you. The person talking about the Shove is living that Shove, and may have some good ideas for how to fix it.

If nothing truly can be done to eliminate or neutralize the Shove, be honest about it. Don't lie and say, "Right, well, it might take me six or eight months to be able to swing that, but I'll work on it," hoping that the Shove will be forgotten. As a rule, unaddressed Shoves don't get forgotten; they just get worse.

Before we move on, I want to address one excuse I hear more than any other for avoiding the Shoves and Tugs conversation: "I don't have the time to sit around with all 10 (or 30, or 50—whatever the number) of my employees and talk about this warm and fuzzy stuff." A productive Shoves and Tugs conversation usually takes 10-20 minutes, less time than you probably spend drinking coffee every day. You don't have to talk to every employee in a single day. Talk to one or two a day, and in a month or so you'll have worked through all 20-40 people. And by the time you reach number 40, you'll already have made some progress retaining the first 20.

TAKING ACTION

The first to-do we suggest is for every manager to create a summary of their conversations. For each employee, we want to know their potential shoves, their potential tugs, and their overall risk for departure – high, medium, and low. We want to identify the issues that need fixing, and if it looks like it will have a positive Return on Investment (ROI), then we're going to do whatever it takes to keep them.

You're probably wondering: *How do I know if something will have a positive ROI?* Essentially, we're going to ask, "Is the cost of losing this person greater than the cost of keeping this person?" The cost of losing somebody can include their relationships, experience, customer bonds, impact on the customer, time and effort to replace them, money to replace them, etc. And the costs of keeping somebody can include everything involved in solving their particular Shove: money, time, resentment from other employees, etc. Typically, the cost of losing someone is much more expensive than the cost of keeping them. So, we're generally going to try and fix their

Shoves. Every so often, it will cost too much to try and fix their Shoves, and in those rare instances, you'll immediately start planning to replace them.

If there's one hallmark of the managers with the best retention rates, the folks who've never lost a high performer, it's their pragmatism. They don't stand on ceremony. When they find a Shove, they fix it. If the Shove is that their leadership style is too micromanaging, they take a leadership course, and they stop micromanaging. If the Shove for one of your high performers is that they're spending too much time working with low performers, they change work assignments or workgroups. In the BrownEx example from the previous chapter, leaders redesigned entire job roles to eliminate a Shove.

By the way, notwithstanding that you're going to hear different answers from every employee, you may start to identify some themes. If there are Shoves endemic to you as a leader, or your department or even your organization, you may hear those. And when you do, they need to be tackled just as swiftly as if it were a solitary issue.

For the Low and Medium departure risks, you've got 30 days to start fixing their Shoves. But if the person is at High risk of departure, you've only got 3 days. If someone is about to quit, or their frustration is off-the-chart, you don't have much time.

High-risk employees are pretty easy to identify. They might just tell you that they're actively considering leaving (or they've actively considered leaving in the past 90 days). Other warning signs include wistful talk about others who have left, becoming withdrawn and not engaging in conversation, acting like they've got something to hide, and more negative comments than you would typically expect from this person.

Once you've eliminated the critical Shoves, take the same approach with the Tugs. Find issues you can tackle that have a positive ROI, and just get going.

The reason why this approach is so effective is that people will tell you exactly why they'll stay and exactly why they'll leave. You don't have to guess; you don't have to spend millions of dollars doing surveys to figure it out. All you have to do is ask a few questions, listen to the answers and take action wherever you can.

PUTTING IT TOGETHER

The final question is, "How did StayHealthy Inc. keep Paul, Christine, Bill, and Sue?" Their manager mapped out all of their Shoves, Tugs, and risk level for leaving, and came up with individual action plans for each of them. They were each interviewed utilizing the Shoves and Tugs Questions and their needs were identified.

Employee	Shoves	Tugs	Risk of Leaving	To D...
Paul	No administrative support	Financial Security/Money	Low	Get F... acces... suppo... for a ... hours... week...
Christine	Group work Repetitive tasks	Creative work Autonomy	Medium	Give Chris... choic... over ... projec... takes Limit with t... Give ... projec... when possi...
Bill	Working late Missing family events	Social Values	Medium	Allow flexib... schec... family event... due a... but al... some worki... from ... Assig... more

				value projec
Sue	Lack of personal space Few chances to lead	Being in charge Leadership	High	Discu track mana positi Trial a team

After interviewing Paul, it appeared that he was pretty content at the moment. He was very motivated by the current pay-for-performance plan and was feeling really positive about his success. His only Shove was a suggestion that he could produce even more if he had some help with his paperwork. In the end, his manager decided that some of the more menial paperwork tasks could be delegated to an intern.

Christine and Bill were more moderate risks. Christine was getting bored with some of the team tasks she was assigned to, and Bill was feeling taxed by the late hours he was putting in that cut into his family time. While team tasks couldn't be eliminated, Christine could be given more choice about which team tasks she preferred to take on. Additionally, she was given a chance to "prove herself" on a new cross-departmental project. Bill was given the option to work from home one day per week, and flexible scheduling was discussed. He was also offered more choices about which projects he preferred.

Sue, on the other hand, was at high risk of leaving. It was discerned that she really wants to move up in the organization, and she sees herself as a leader. She likes to be "in charge" and has worked extremely well as a leader. But she's had few opportunities to lead. She also disliked her cubicle arrangement with its lack of privacy. Since Sue has good potential as a leader, it was discussed with her that she could be put up for promotion if she demonstrates excellent productivity and leadership skills over the next six months. A promotion would mean a managerial position and a private office. Her manager spelled out very clearly what Sue would need to do and how she would need to act.

In sum, maximizing the Tugs and minimizing the Shoves keep employees tied to their organization. Each person has their own unique Shoves and Tugs, and these Shoves and

Tugs are not static. What StayHealthy, Inc. has shown us is that "One Size Fits One" and that, like our waistlines over the years, sizes are always changing.

For More Information

For free downloadable resources including quizzes, handouts, and discussion guides, please visit:
www.leadershipiq.com/EmployeeRetentionBook

DEADLY SIN #3
Not Listening Deeply

CONDUCTING THE SHOVES AND TUGS conversations taught in the previous chapter will test every leader's ability to listen deeply and empathically. It's not enough to ask employees what's demotivating them; we have to truly hear and internalize their responses. So in this chapter, you'll learn techniques and research to dramatically increase your ability to listen deeply, empathically, and without defensiveness.

WATCH FOR THESE THREE WARNING SIGNS OF INEFFECTIVE SHOVES AND TUGS CONVERSATIONS

Shoves and Tugs conversations should be a required activity for every leader. This conversation is the fastest and least expensive method for assessing and improving employee retention, employee motivation, and spotting burnout. Plus, given the direct and uncomplicated nature of the activity (it's literally just a conversation between two people), it should be fairly straightforward to implement successfully.

Yet the data tells us that notwithstanding their putative simplicity, the typical one-on-one meeting is not delivering much value. Following the Shoves and Tugs script in the previous chapter will obviously improve the conversations dramatically. But even with that script, it's still important to evaluate the success of our conversations.

In the Leadership IQ study, The State Of Leadership Development, we learned that if leaders respond constructively when employees share their work problems, those employees are 12 times more likely to recommend the company as a great employer. Here's the issue: Only 26% of employees say that their leader always responds constructively when they share their work problems.

Think about how many problems, big or small, an employee could face on a daily basis. From time management to conflicts, from hybrid working to impossible deadlines, there's no shortage of problems facing today's employees. If a leader listens to those concerns without shooting the messenger, getting defensive, or denying reality, employee retention skyrockets.

How can you quickly pinpoint whether or why Shoves and Tugs conversations are underperforming? Just pay attention to these three warning signs.

Warning Sign #1: It's a Monologue, Not a Dialogue

Shoves and Tugs conversations should not be a forum for managers to speak *at* their employees; that's a monologue. Instead, these interactions are dialogues, speaking with their employees. There should be an equal exchange of information, both parties should learn something about the other, and there will ideally be as many questions as statements.

Far too many managers enter into Shoves and Tugs conversations with an interminable agenda of items they want to share with their people. However, this is a terrible format for one-way information sharing. Memos, town halls, and video recordings are all faster and cheaper ways to disseminate information. Shoves and Tugs conversations' key benefit is that the manager will learn something new about the employee's motivators, demotivators, goals, etc. Only with this new information will the manager learn how to retain them (and unleash the employee's full potential and unlock their growth).

Warning Sign #2: You Don't Learn About Employees' Demotivators

Any time a manager talks with an employee, the manager should learn something about the employee's motivation. What work do they enjoy most? What was their proudest moment this past month? What excites them about their job? In what areas do they want to grow and develop?

But there's another requirement for successful Shoves and Tugs conversations — learning about what demotivates the employee. It's wonderful to learn what excites someone, but what about that person's frustrations and disappointments? All those exciting projects and enjoyable workgroups won't matter much if an employee is furious because they're feeling slighted or their boss won't listen to their great ideas. How can an employee grow and develop when they can't resolve their biggest frustrations?

This means, of course, that managers need to ask their people directly, "Could you tell me about a time in the past month when you felt frustrated or demotivated or burned out?" After the leader has inquired about growth opportunities and inspiring moments, they must tackle the demotivators.

Think of it like this: If you've got dinner reservations at a hip new outdoor restaurant tonight, will you enjoy your meal if you spent the last two hours at work livid or despondent? It's hard to enjoy cool new experiences when frustrations loom large in our minds.

WARNING SIGN #3: YOU HEAR SUPERFICIAL RESPONSES

Imagine that you asked an employee to describe a recent time when they got frustrated at work. Now imagine they say, "Nah, that never happens to me, I'm all good." Would you believe them? What if they answered, "Maybe there was something this month, but why do you want to know?" Do you think they trust you?

As we learned in the last chapter, those answers are superficial and suspicious, respectively. And both answers are indicative of a trust problem. If Shoves and Tugs conversations are not a routine activity at your organization, it's possible that the first few attempts will engender some superficiality and suspicion. While there isn't much that can immediately convince an employee to trust and disclose, people will see the leader's positive intent and progressively open up over subsequent months.

USE THIS ONE SENTENCE TO IMMEDIATELY BECOME A MORE EMPATHIC LISTENER

Shoves and Tugs conversations work best when leaders and employees have a deep connection built on empathy. What builds that empathic connection? The list is nearly endless, but one characteristic that is virtually guaranteed to build a connection is when others feel that we truly understand them. That can be as simple as uttering the sentence, "I can really put myself in your shoes." As you're going to see, that sentence is actually backed by research.

Perspective-taking, as it's technically known, generally shows up when we're in conversation with another person. If we're talking to a friend, colleague, boss, etc., and they feel like we have truly put ourselves in their shoes, they're most likely going to connect with us.

Now, we're not talking about some bad caricature of active listening, where we nod vigorously and mindlessly grunt 'uh-huh,' 'sure,' 'I see…' and so on because that is not perspective-taking or listening empathetically.

Perspective-taking is seeing the world, or a particular situation, from another person's viewpoint. Atticus Finch, the moral guide and conscience in Harper Lee's To Kill A Mockingbird, sets perspective-taking as a key life lesson for his daughter when he tells her "You never really understand a person until you consider things from his point of view . . . until you climb into his skin and walk around in it." George Herbert Mead, the great American philosopher, called perspective-taking "the capacity to take the role of the other and to adopt alternative perspectives vis a vis oneself." And the legendary psychologist Carl Rogers said it's to "perceive the internal frame of reference of another with accuracy, and with the emotional components and meanings which pertain thereto, as if one were the person, but without ever losing the 'as if condition."

Now, there are quite a few people who could use some help with perspective-taking. Across the thousands of people who've taken the online test "Do You

Know How To Listen With Empathy?" about a third of respondents failed pretty badly. And only about 20% of people achieved perfect scores. So we've still got some room to grow.

One of the most important studies on perspective-taking comes from a team of researchers at UCLA. They conducted six different experiments to assess what happens when a person feels like someone took their perspective. No surprise, every single experiment found that people feel great when someone takes their perspective. Several of the experiments didn't even tell subjects that the other person was successful in taking their perspective (e.g., maybe they tried but failed to put themselves into our shoes). But it didn't matter. As long as subjects believed that the other person made an effort to try, they experienced more liking, empathy, and generosity towards the perspective taker.

After a few of those experiments, the researchers took it a step further. Subjects were asked to write an essay describing a time a boss had treated them unfairly. Believing that another person was reading their essay (it was really just the researchers), one group of subjects was told that the reader said, "I tried to take their perspective, but I just couldn't put myself in their shoes."

The other group was told the reader said, "I tried to take their perspective, and I could really put myself in their shoes." When people heard that the reader had successfully taken their perspective, they liked that person 19% more. And they felt 78% more empathy towards them.

If you're wondering whether any of this led to tangible benefits, all subjects were told that they would be playing a game with the reader. They were informed that whoever won the game would be entered into a drawing to win money and that the person who went first in the game had the best chance of winning. The researchers then offered the subjects the choice of whether they wanted to go first (and be more likely to win money) or give up their turn to the reader (and be less likely to win money). The subjects who were told that the reader successfully took their perspective were 59% more likely to give up their turn (and cost themselves a better chance of winning money)! And all because they believed that reader took their perspective.

If you can take another person's perspective—if you stand in their shoes and see the world through their eyes—the odds of them connecting with you skyrocket. As you might imagine, this is absolutely essential when you're conducting a Shoves and Tugs conversation.

If you remember nothing else from this section, when you have your next Shoves and Tugs conversation, try using the phrase "I can really put myself in your shoes."

Watch Out for Two Phrases That Signal We're not Listening

Sadly, we've all had (or are having) the experience of a boss who doesn't listen to us. And we're not talking about really blatant situations (e.g., they literally turn away from us or roll their eyes), but rather those situations in which the boss acts like they're listening but hears nothing we say. It's pretty easy to imagine how quickly that could ruin a Shoves and Tugs conversation.

We recently witnessed just such a case. An executive, let's call him Pat, was holding a town hall meeting to discuss the company's recent, and disappointing, employee engagement survey results.

About 40 employees showed up to the meeting. He kicked things off by saying, "Welcome everybody. As you know, I'm having this meeting today because I want to hear your concerns, frustrations and demotivators directly. I'm here to listen about your issues with your supervisors, so fire away."

One employee raised his hand first and said, "With the recent cost-cutting, I think we've all got concerns about whether we're going to have jobs next year." Pat quickly responded, "Oh, I hear you. You think you've got problems? At least your wages are ones that other companies will pay. But I'm the VP, and I'm over 50, so when you combine my high salary with my age, I'm going to have a really tough time finding a job. But hey, life's not fair, right?"

Then another employee raised their hand. "I actually have a different concern. My supervisor tells me that I'm supposed to bring her any suggestions for improvement, but when I do, it's like she doesn't listen to me." Pat responded, "I know how that feels, but I don't want you to worry, because those feelings will pass and you will get over it."

You can imagine how quickly employee participation died after hearing those two phrases from their executive. Because among the quickest ways a boss can dismiss employees' concerns, and show they're not listening, is to say two phrases: "Life's not fair" and "You'll get over it."

There are a lot of ways to not listen or respond poorly to employee concerns, so what makes those two phrases especially bad?

Phrase #1: "Life's not Fair"

This phrase is telling employees that sure, bad stuff happens, and we all have some feelings about that, but I don't really care to hear about the bad things that are happening to you. Just accept that bad things happen and get on with your life. It's a way of telling someone that 'I don't want to hear about your problems.'

Phrase #2: "You'll Get Over It"

Few phrases are as blatantly unempathic as this one. It's essentially saying, "You don't need to share your issues with me because if you wait long enough, you'll just stop having any feelings about it."

Now, some grizzled leaders sometimes ask, "does listening and responding constructively really matter?" Well, going back to Leadership IQ's study, The State Of Leadership Development, if leaders respond constructively when employees share their work problems, those employees are 12 times more likely to recommend the company as a great employer.

Are there times when life isn't fair? Or when we do need to get over things? Of course. But when someone, especially an employee, is sharing a problem with us, they need to be heard, not dismissed. It destroys an employee's motivation when their boss dismisses them.

TEST FOR BURNOUT IN YOUR SHOVES AND TUGS CONVERSATIONS

A benefit of listening deeply during Shoves and Tugs conversations is that you'll likely spot when employees are suffering from burnout. The language we use reveals a lot about our mental state. And whether we say those words out loud or just in our heads, you can diagnose when your employees are suffering from burnout just by taking careful note of the words they choose.

Employee burnout is highly correlated with employee resignations. And even if an employee doesn't overtly resign, burnout can be a harbinger of Quiet Quitting. Not all burned-out employees will stop giving extra effort, but spotting the signs of burnout gives you the chance to solve real issues for your employees, reduce their pain, alleviate burnout, and retain them.

Here are five words and some synonyms that are red flags for feelings of burnout; listen for these words in your Shoves and Tugs conversations.

Exhausted (Fried, Burned Out)

One of the most obvious words that people suffering from burnout use is exhausted. Exhausted, and synonyms like fried or burnt or burned out, convey a much deeper and more emotional fatigue than simply being tired.

Anyone who's had a bad night's sleep trudges through the next day tired. But exhausted conveys a deeper sense that our psychological resources like optimism and resilience have been drained. And if you're feeling like your resilience is running on empty lately, you're not alone. According to the tens of thousands of people who have taken Leadership IQ's Resiliency Test, fewer than a quarter of people have high resilience at present.

Unproductive (Not Accomplishing Anything)

The data from Leadership IQ's online time management test shows that around two-thirds of people say, "I often leave work wondering 'did I actually accomplish anything today?'"

Feeling unproductive (and saying to ourselves, "I'm not getting anything done lately") is a classic sign of burnout. When our emotional reserves are high, and we're achieving big goals left and right, we're highly unlikely to grumble about our lack of productivity. But when we're burned out, it's quite easy to have days where we feel as though we're running through quicksand; no matter how many hours we've logged, a feeling of accomplishment eludes us.

Can't (Unable)

Do you believe that you control your own success and destiny? Or do you feel like events outside your control could prevent you from being successful?

The underlying belief here is your locus of control. People with an internal locus of control believe that they control their own success or failure; those with an external locus of control attribute success or failure to factors outside of their control.

Words like "can't" or "unable" can often indicate an external locus of control. When I say, "I can't get anything done at work because my colleagues don't pull their weight," we're relinquishing control of our career to our colleagues. But for someone with an internal locus of control, while it may be true that our coworkers are subpar, there are still actions that I can take to improve my situation. In a Leadership IQ study, we discovered that only 17% of people have a high internal locus of control. This matters because people with a high internal locus of control are 136% happier with their careers.

Impossible (Never, no Way)

When we feel burned out, it's common for our language to evidence more negativity and emotionality. For example, when we're not suffering burnout, we might say, "this project is going to be challenging." But when we're fried or exhausted, we might say, "this project is impossible," or "I'll never finish in time."

Words like "impossible" and "never" are called absolutes. They represent a form of black-and-white thinking, and it's a well-known cognitive distortion. Most situations in life are subtle shades of grey, not black-and-white. The project may be challenging, but is it truly impossible?

The more someone engages in absolutist (black-and-white) thinking, the less likely they are to see hidden opportunities or possibilities. That can lead directly to feelings of despair and hopelessness, which only furthers feelings of burnout.

MEH (BLAH, MALAISE, HOPELESS)

Of course, "meh" isn't really proper English, but it's a commonly used, and incredibly descriptive, word. And frankly, very few people are walking around talking about their current sense of malaise.

Regardless of the exact word we use, we're really talking about a loss of optimism, and that loss of optimism is pretty widespread right now. Through several of our studies, we've discovered that only 13% of people have a high level of optimism, while nearly 33% of people have low or moderately low optimism.

The problem for businesses is that optimistic employees are 103% more inspired to give their best effort at work. And if employees aren't giving their best effort, most companies are going to struggle.

Optimism isn't just for businesses; it actually affects our health. Among the numerous studies on optimism that prove its benefits, one evaluated middle-aged patients scheduled to undergo coronary artery bypass surgery. Six months after surgery, researchers found that optimists were only half as likely as pessimists to require re-hospitalization.

If you start to pay close attention to the words coming out of your employees' mouths, you're going to catch the warning signs of nascent or full-blown burnout.

BEWARE OF TOXIC POSITIVITY

Do you ever feel like your organization's leaders are trying too hard to pretend that everything's just fine? Or that company-wide memos avoid any topic that can't be positively spun? Or that uncomfortable conversations are muzzled with warnings like, "let's not dwell on the negative"? If any of those scenarios feel familiar, you've likely suffered toxic positivity.

Toxic positivity is an excessive and distorted form of positive thinking. It's putting a positive spin on all experiences, no matter how dire or tragic. For example, you could be experiencing toxic positivity when a friend or boss minimizes or refuses to acknowledge your negative feelings. Or perhaps they go further and try to spin your dire situation in a positive way, like 'this is a blessing in disguise' or 'all things happen for a reason.'

Toxic positivity is not optimism; the belief outcomes of events or experiences will generally be good or positive. Optimism doesn't involve denying unpleasant realities; in fact, optimism is often most evident in how people respond to hardship or adversity.

Toxic positivity in organizations is often seen when leaders avoid sharing or discussing the tough challenges they're facing. Or when leaders don't want to hear about employees' demotivators (aka Shoves).

There's a long-standing belief among many leaders that talking about tough issues scares people and worsens the situation. The reality is quite the opposite. In a study, called The Risks Of Ignoring Employee Feedback, we found that if an employee believes their company openly discusses their challenges, they're about ten times more likely to recommend it as a great employer.

To avoid toxic positivity, leaders and companies need to accept that their employees are not clueless. Nor are their people so fragile that they can't handle reality. In fact, ignoring or dismissing reality is one of the fastest ways to undermine employees' trust in leadership. Instead, leaders need to acknowledge reality (like Shoves) and then focus their efforts making that reality better.

When leaders avoid sharing tough challenges or use phrases like, "everything happens for a reason" or "this is a blessing in disguise," not only are they denying reality, they're also evidencing a lack of empathy.

Of course, people are hurting and burned out right now. Shoves are everywhere. Denying that pain, however, is not going to magically dissipate it. The best leaders will accept and acknowledge reality and then work hard to improve it.

PUTTING IT TOGETHER

To really make Shoves and Tugs conversation work, leaders need to listen deeply to their employees' concerns. That means taking employees' perspectives, making conversations about their issues not ours, being vigilant for signs of burnout, and ensuring this is truly a dialogue and not a chance for us to talk at our people.

DEADLY SIN #4
Overcomplicating Your Solutions

ONCE YOU'VE DISCOVERED EACH OF your employees' Shoves and Tugs, you're ready to start taking action. In many cases, the fix for removing Shoves and adding Tugs will be self-evident. In fact, your employees will often tell you specifically what needs to be done.

It's a mistake to overthink this. Imagine your star employee's biggest frustration is being micromanaged; specifically, being forced to check in every hour with status updates. You don't need a major process or task force to fix this Shove; just stop micromanaging. Make the check-ins every few hours or twice a day instead of every hour. Or whatever.

Whether the issue is a Shove or a Tug, much of the time the solutions are straightforward. To help you move even more quickly in addressing your team's Shoves and Tugs, the rest of this chapter contains quickly implementable techniques for addressing a number of common Shoves and Tugs.

GIVE MORE POSITIVE REINFORCEMENT

High performers need positive feedback; they do a great job, and they should have that acknowledged. And a lack of positive reinforcement is a well-established Shove for many employees (especially top performers).

However, phrases like "great job" or "nice work" are so vague as to be virtually useless. And in some cases, they may even do harm.

Let's imagine that one of your high performers just did a great job on a report. What made their work great? Well, perhaps they got it done three days ahead of schedule. Maybe they added some extra data analyses that you hadn't thought to request.

Now, your high performer has just done great and hard work, with extra effort and creativity, and we come along and say, "great job". There are a few problems with that. First, it sounds like we don't understand everything the high performer accomplished (i.e., beat the deadline and made a better report). Second, it can sound like we don't appreciate everything they accomplished. Third, the phrase 'great job' has little pedagogical value. It doesn't teach the high performer which of their terrific behaviors you would like to see repeated in the future (beating deadlines and adding extra analyses).

So what could you say instead of "great job"? Try this: Pat, the way you got that report done three days ahead of schedule means a lot to the customer and to me. And the extra data analyses you did were really creative and added a lot of value to the report because you discovered the root cause of the customer's issues. Thank you.

That little script takes more time than saying "great job." But isn't that extra 60 seconds worth it? You just showed that you understand and appreciate the particulars of their accomplishments and you told your high performer exactly what they should keep doing in the future. That's quite a bit of value for an extra 60 seconds of effort.

Unfortunately, in one of Leadership IQ's recent studies, 61% of employees said their boss does a lousy job of recognizing and acknowledging their accomplishments. For example, we recently got an email from a retail worker who shared that a customer wrote a letter to his store commending the worker's performance. His boss put the letter in with his paycheck. But he never said a word about it.

You don't need to blow constant smoke to keep your high performers motivated. In fact, doling out meaningless praise is guaranteed to work against you. But if you offer specific positive reinforcement when warranted, you'll keep your high performers inspired, and you'll actually increase the frequency of their high performer behavior.

There is a psychological phenomenon that helps explain why many managers don't recognize, let alone praise, employees' great work. It's called reason-based choice (from the research paper

"Reason-based choice" by Eldar Shafir, Itamar Simonson, and Amos Tversky), and it works like this:

Using an experiment from the paper, imagine that you're a juror in a child custody case following a messy divorce, and you have to award/deny sole custody to one of the parents. You decide to base your decision entirely on the following few observations:

- **Parent A has:**
  - average income
  - average health
  - average working hours
  - reasonable rapport with child
  - relatively stable social life
- **Parent B has:**
  - above average income
  - very close relationship with the child
  - extremely active social life
  - lots of work-related travel
  - minor health problems

Now, imagine that you're asked, "To which parent would you award sole custody of the child?" In the actual experiment, 64% of the subjects saw Parent B as the better choice. Why? Probably because Parent B has 'above average income' and a 'very close relationship with the child.'

But now imagine that you're asked, "To which parent would you deny sole custody of the child?" Shockingly, 55% still chose Parent B! Why? Well, notwithstanding their positive attributes, Parent B also has an 'extremely active social life,' 'lots of work-related travel, and 'minor health problems.'

One of the big lessons from this is that if you're looking for reasons to award custody, you're likely to focus on Parent B's positive attributes. If you're looking for reasons to deny custody, you're likely to focus on Parent B's negative attributes. The phrasing of the choice biases us towards focusing on and using some information more than others. Or put even more simply, if we're looking for reasons to choose or award somebody, we're going to focus on positive things. If we're looking for reasons to deny or censure somebody, we're going to focus on negative things.

So what does reason-based choice have to do with giving compliments to our employees? First, we have to think about the mindset that many leaders bring to the workplace. Are they wandering around the office looking for reasons why people are doing great work and things are going right? Or are they wandering around looking for mistakes and reasons why things are going wrong?

The average leader spends more time looking for reasons why things are not working (the negative issues) than they are looking for all the reasons why things are going well. So, much like the juror in the study, if leaders are looking for reasons to 'deny,' they'll likely miss all the positive ('award') things that are happening.

As an example, think about the last project status meeting you attended. If it was like the typical meeting, there was a lot of time spent discussing how things are falling behind (or are at risk of doing so), the risk points, scenarios for mitigating time and money overruns, and all sorts of negative topics. There probably wasn't a whole lot of time spent going around the room looking for all the wonderful things that have been happening.

What reason-based choice tells us is that if we spend our time at work looking for problems (e.g., reasons to deny custody), we're going to find a lot of problems. And if we spend our time looking for positive things (e.g., reasons to award custody), we're going to find many more examples of people doing great work.

Every leader has a choice as they go through their days; are they looking for reasons to 'deny' or to 'award'? If leaders adopt the common 'deny' approach, they'll keep finding all sorts of reasons why things aren't working. But if they make the conscious choice to look for reasons to 'award,' they'll be way more likely to recognize (and compliment) all the great work that their employees are performing, and that is likely to result in a significantly more engaged and inspired workforce.

Give Employees a Chance to Lead

For a number of employees, being in charge or having a chance to lead is a big Tug. But a lot of leaders get uncomfortable when faced with identifying and training the people who might someday replace them. It can be tough to admit, but fear of being rendered useless can make leaders territorial; they keep for themselves all the juicy projects that encourage growth on the job, secretly afraid to share and to let others shine. Or they claim they're so busy leading the organization's success that there's just no time to train anyone for succession.

As a general rule, if you don't have 2 or 3 succession planning candidates for most key leadership or management positions coming up, it's time to fix that. Start by applying these 3 categories of succession planning assessment to the people you lead. For best results, these metrics should be updated yearly:

Category 1: Ready Now: These are the folks who are ready to be leaders. They should be considered for the best positions and assignments coming available.

Category 2: Ready Soon: With the help of some leadership development opportunities (so don't hog all the cool assignments for yourself) these folks will soon make the leap to "Ready Now."

Category 3: Keep Watching: These folks need some nudging with developmental activities and mentoring.

We created the 'Manager for a Day' Program to help take the sting out of succession planning by inviting 'Ready Now' category employees to ride shotgun. It's a fairly painless (and free) technique that gives you an extra set of hands, develops self-sufficiency in your high-performing employees, and gives these potential succession candidates a critical appreciation of management roles.

And, of course, it's a major Tug for those employees who aspire to leadership roles.

The extra time with the boss also increases employee engagement. In a recent Leadership IQ study, we found that most people spend only half the time they should be spending with their boss. But people who spend the optimal 6 hours per week interacting with their direct leader are 29% more inspired, 30% more engaged, 16% more innovative, and 15% more intrinsically motivated than those who spend only one hour per week. That's true even when employees don't like the boss!

Getting the Manager for a Day Program rolling is easy. Once you identify your Ready Now employees, say to them, "One day a week I'm going to have each of you work with me. You're going to shadow me and start to take over some of the management activities that I might otherwise do." So if you have five really great high performers who have good leadership potential, you'll give Bob Monday, Sally Tuesday, Frank Wednesday, Jane Thursday, and so on.

You'll say, "Okay, Bob, on Mondays, you're going to work with me on ABC management activity. Sally, you're going to work with me on Tuesdays on XYZ management activity, et cetera."

The Manager for a Day Program accomplishes a couple of things. Number one, it gives these high-performing employees in the Ready Now category a taste of what it's like to actually perform in a management role. Management activities are often quite different than individual contributor activities. Organizations will often promote folks, assigning them to a multi-person team when all they know is how to be an individual contributor. It's a setup for failure.

Manager for a Day helps to ease potential new managers into the job, providing a little sampling, a realistic preview that gives Ready Now level employees a flavor for the job. And you're going to find that once they get a taste for the job, not everybody actually wants to be a manager (even if they originally identified being a leader as a Tug). Not everybody wants to take that next level up in the corporate hierarchy, and that's good information to have.

Having your best people working alongside you as Manager for a Day also helps alleviate that wonky feeling about succession that invites territorial behavior. It creates a safe space that allows you to become a lot more comfortable delegating. If you just take succession planning in the abstract and try to deduce who could potentially fill your job, the natural human reaction is, "I'll tell you who could fill my job. Me! I fill my job. I don't want anyone else to fill my job." But when you start to involve your best people working alongside you, it makes you a lot more comfortable with this person as you start to see the role they can fill and how they work in that role. When you have your 3, 4, or 5 best people helping you out, your job gets a lot easier as well!

Manager for a Day helps develop our talent pool for succession. It also works when you don't want or need a full-time manager, as a high performer reward (gives high performers a taste of management), and for easing new managers into the job.

If you've noticed that some of your employees view leadership as a major Tug, try a Manager for a Day program. Take your best folks in the Ready Now category and try it for a few months. See how people react. Find out who likes being in a management job and who doesn't. Manager for a Day is a simple, cheap, easy way of identifying future leadership talent.

MAKE A PERSONAL CONNECTION

Recently, a newly-hired manager sent us this note about how he was able to connect with his new employees, even though they were bitter and cynical because of their previous leaders (who were awful). We're sharing this letter because it shows you how employee retention can sometimes be a simple task if you're willing to exert just a little bit of personal energy, attention, and time.

Dear Leadership IQ,

I wanted to share this technique because I think it could really benefit your readers. I just joined this company a year ago and I was hired to oversee a large team. This team previously had three managers in two years, the lowest employee engagement scores in the company, and obscenely high employee turnover. In all of my previous leadership roles, retention has always been a priority and top of mind. One of my strategies is to connect individually with as many team members as possible and attempt to create a professional/personal relationship. Honestly, it was hard with this team because they were so bitter and cynical after all of their bad experiences with the previous terrible leaders.

During my first two months on the job, I noticed a large number of my technical team sporting Pink Floyd t-shirts from time to time. As I'm always looking to engage them on something other than a professional level, I began searching for a hook that I could use to initiate a conversation with them. That hook came when I learned of a Pink Floyd Tribute band that had scheduled a performance in town. I looked up some information about the band and asked those I had observed wearing the shirts if they were familiar with the band. The conversation led to a general discussion of the music they were interested in. That initial discussion has since evolved into other areas, family, work, their concerns, suggestions, feedback, and even compliments. This technique could include anything that is of interest to them. Once you figure out their interests, educate yourself a bit on the subject and look for a hook to initiate a conversation. The key, I believe, is to avoid the obvious, like talking about major or local sporting events or the weather, and really scout for their niche interests. That's where you will get the best bang for the buck.

In my experience, you need to move the relationship from one that is strictly professional to one that is professional/personal. The kind where your team sees you as someone who cares about more than just their production. The differentiation is that you, as an employer, are a "kindred spirit" with similar interests. With that belief, they are much less likely to accept another position unless it's truly a much better opportunity. I know this works because our employee turnover has dropped by a huge 83% in my first 12 months on the job. We just completed our first employee engagement survey since I took over, and our overall scores are up by more than 40%. We've still got a lot of work to do, but my boss tells me that he's never seen my department this engaged. Thank you for letting me share.

Bill

First, we're very grateful to Bill for sharing his story. Second, what's clear from his letter is that it didn't take much at all for Bill to break through the bitterness and cynicism felt by these employees. What it took was genuine interest, caring, and a willingness to engage with people directly. And, of course, it takes a little extra time.

It can be hard for leaders to find the time to interact with their staff; we've got reports, meetings, proposals, calls, and a million other things to do. But Bill would never have gained the Pink Floyd insight if he wasn't out of his office, interacting with his people. While bonding over Pink Floyd certainly won't work for everybody (even bonding over music might not work), there are thousands of potential connections that a leader could make with their employees. Those connections, in turn, are the key to deepening your relationships with your employees.

DRASTICALLY INCREASE EMPLOYEES' LEARNING

A Leadership IQ study, called If They're Not Learning Then You're Not Leading, discovered that employees who are always learning new things at work are ten times more likely to feel inspired to give their best effort than people who never learn new skills at work.

However, while every company has seen this research, the majority aren't doing very much to foster significant learning. This is true even when their employees say that learning and growth is a major Tug.

If organizations do encourage employee growth and learning, rarely do they put much executive muscle behind that encouragement. But it's really not that hard to do. For example, AnswerConnect, a company of nearly 2,000 people, has paid learning time. It's 150 minutes a week for full-time employees, and to achieve the best results in terms of learning, retention, skills development, etc., they want people doing this every day for 30 minutes. As their CEO Natalie Ruiz told us, "Whether salaried or hourly, people just schedule their learning time into their day and block their schedules accordingly."

And be sure to let your employees scratch virtually any intellectual itch. You don't want employees watching Netflix for 30 minutes, of course, but do give them the freedom to learn in new areas. As Ruiz explains, "Let's say your position is in HR, but you're really interested in marketing or finance. We think that's great, and for 30 minutes a day, you can learn anything and everything you want on those topics."

The more your folks are learning and engaged, the more likely they are to stay. And if they're developing skills in new areas, they could also be positioning themselves for career growth in other departments in your company.

Leadership IQ's study, The State Of Leadership Development, discovered that only 20% of employees say that their leader always takes an active role in helping them grow and develop their full potential. There are hundreds of ways to help someone develop their potential, but giving them paid time to learn every single day is a wonderful place to start.

A big plus of this approach is that it ensures that learning always happens, even when someone is having one of those insanely busy, four-alarm types of days. When your schedule is packed beyond belief, among the first activities that get discarded are the ones that fall under the heading of personal growth. But when that learning is built into the daily routine, it ensures that growth is prioritized.

GIVE SOME UNUSUAL GIFTS

In the Leadership IQ study, The State Of Employee Burnout, we learned that only 25% of leaders feel that their employees are thriving emotionally and mentally and that 79% of leaders have seen less productivity as a result of employee burnout.

But what are the Shoves underlying all that pain? Is it that people are overworked due to staffing shortages? Is it that employees are struggling to work from home effectively while having their kids around? Is it trying to maintain a household while still doing their jobs? Are they frustrated with their weight and health?

It's likely that across your workforce, you've got employees who are frustrated with all those issues and dozens more. The challenge is to assess and diagnose Shoves that are most impacting your unique workforce.

Most companies, unfortunately, take a guess as to what their employees might enjoy. And that's how so many organizations end up giving their employees generic gift cards or fruit baskets or whatever.

While it's not wrong to give employees holiday gifts or offer benefits that could attract and retain employees, organizations should try to target these offerings to deliver maximum benefit to the well-being of their people.

If you discovered that a large number of employees were struggling with household chores while working from home, you might consider offering employees a subscription to a cleaning service. If it's more an issue of trying to maintain family rhythms with long hours, perhaps a food delivery membership would be more appropriate. If you hear frustrations about health, you might consider gym memberships or emotional wellness classes. If the top concern is a lack of career advancement, educational reimbursement might be the way to go.

None of those benefits and gifts are good or bad; their efficacy will depend entirely on the context of your particular employee population and what you learn in your shoves and Tugs conversations.

STOP THE BUTT-IN-SEAT MENTALITY

There's an insidious attitude permeating many companies; that when employees have their butts in their seats, it means they're productive. But if you've ever seen studies on actual employee productivity, or if you've ever forced yourself to sit at your desk for eight straight hours, you know that having a butt-in-the-seat does not equal productivity. The problem becomes especially acute when the butt-in-seat mentality follows remote employees into their home workspace.

With so many people working remotely these days, leaders need to deeply understand the Shoves associated with being remote.

A study from RescueTime found that knowledge workers check email and Slack every six minutes, with more than a third checking email or Slack every three minutes. And 40% of knowledge workers never get more than 30 minutes straight of focused time. The email interruptions and lack of straight focus time help explain why knowledge workers, on average, have just 2 hours and 48 minutes a day for productive tasks. That can become a major Shove, especially for people working remotely.

Time chunking (also known as time blocking) is essentially carving out pieces of the day when you can disconnect from email (or Slack or IM, etc.) and focus on performing work that requires deep thinking. It's not a complicated concept, and you've no doubt experienced the drastic productivity improvements that time chunking creates. It's just like when you work from a coffee shop and accomplish more in one hour than you would have accomplished in eight hours at the office.

If you want to drastically improve the productivity of your remote team, and remove a major Shove, start giving your team dedicated blocks of time throughout the day when they have to be online and other times when they can disconnect and work free from interruptions.

For example, you could set core periods throughout the day, e.g., 10 AM-12 PM and 2 PM-4 PM, when employees have to be accessible online (via email, Slack, IM, etc.). You could even add these three sentences to your work-from-home policy:

> *Employees must be available to their supervisors and co- workers during core work hours. There are two core periods each day. The first runs from 10 AM – 12 PM and the second from 2 PM – 4 PM.*

Making this kind of policy change offers several benefits: First, you're giving your employees periods of the day when they're allowed to disconnect, to focus deeply on their work without interruptions, and actually produce great results.

Second, having times throughout the day when they can disconnect allows your remote employees that have kids to connect with their family. It can be chaotic having kids and spouses around. But when your employees have an hour to disconnect from email and check in with everyone in the house, they'll likely be able to restore some semblance of order. That means when they come back to their desk, they'll be significantly more focused and productive.

Third, there's much to be said for focusing on the results someone achieves rather than how long they sit in front of a computer. When we're operating with a butt-in-seat mentality, we're de facto telling people, "it's not what you get done but how long you sit there that matters." There are organizations where employees are online for three hours a day that accomplish twice as much work as companies where everyone is online for ten straight hours.

Finally, when your employees get to disconnect for a few hours a day to accomplish deep-thinking work, guess who else gets to unplug and enjoy similar accomplishments? You! It's an absolute treat for most leaders to have a few hours when they know that they won't be interrupted and, thus, can produce better and faster results.

PUTTING IT TOGETHER

This chapter is not intended to make you implement every one of these techniques. Rather, it's an assemblage of techniques from which you can pick and choose depending on the Shoves and Tugs you're addressing. If your team is suffering from a lack of recognition, use the positive reinforcement technique. If your employees are burning out from a butt-in-seat mindset, then use that technique. And so on.

The key is to let your Shoves and Tugs conversations dictate which techniques to try. Don't mechanically cycle through every technique in this chapter; let your employees tell you which ones would be most beneficial.

DEADLY SIN #5
Neglecting The First 90 Days

IMAGINE YOU'RE THE VICE PRESIDENT of Sales at a large international ad agency. You just hired Roger, who was a high-performing salesman at a small local agency. He came from a small, personal environment, where he was the top dog. Now he needs to navigate the bureaucracy of your large firm and start out at the bottom. As you walk him into your office and remember the nightmare that was your first month on the job here, you wonder if Roger is going to stay or bolt. What can you do to make the transition easier for Roger? How do you keep him from running?

The reality is that turnover rates in the first 90 days are higher than for any other period of employment. Leadership IQ studies have found a wide range of early turnover, from as low as 2% to as high as 50% in some companies. Our studies also found that companies whose leaders focus on building bonds with their employees in the first 90 days retain more employees during that initial period and tend to retain them longer overall. What we have learned from those companies is to *put out the welcome mat* and *bring them into the fold.*

PUT OUT THE WELCOME MAT

Before your new hire even steps through the door, you want them to feel welcomed, wanted, and prepared from the start of their career at your organization. Before day one comes, send a card. Given our propensity for card-driven holidays, you probably won't be shocked to learn that some stores sell a "Welcome" card for new employees. Get or make a card, get all your employees to sign it, and send it to your new employee's home.

We know sending physical mail seems old school, and that's why we recommend it. It's done so rarely in our high-tech world that this one simple gesture stands out and builds your new hire's excitement for joining your team. You'll also reduce any regrets they may have had about quitting their previous job. Finally, if they don't live alone, you'll start to win over their spouse, partner, or roommates (a critical, and usually ignored, factor in every employee's decision-making about whether to join or leave an organization).

When you're excited and/or anxious about a new situation, do you conduct some extra research? If you're about to take your first African safari, wouldn't you buy some travel books and do some reading? Or spend a few hours Googling African safaris? Of course you would, and that's just how your new employees feel (in fact, starting a new job is a lot like a safari). So this is a great time to give them some of the key reading materials – the handbook, any marketing materials, the policies and procedures. Because they're excited, and a little anxious, they're much more likely to read now than they are at any other point in employment. And this will make them feel a little better.

Another great idea is to assemble a roster of your current team. Don't make it too serious or intimidating, but provide a basic "who's who." The best ones we've seen include everyone's name, title, years of service, one sentence about their job functions, and then something off-the-wall like their favorite tree or vacation or food. The trick is to give the new employee something really memorable to read, and nothing accomplishes that like humor. It also disarms them and makes your staff seem approachable.

Also, tell your employees that a new employee is joining the team. It's truly remarkable how many managers forget to tell their current employees that a new employee is arriving. So prep them. Schedule meetings with all of your team members, and make sure that every current employee attends. In the meeting, you need to prep current staff and assuage whatever fears and anxieties they may have. You want to make sure that the team is going to be friendly and helpful, not unwelcoming and antagonistic.

First impressions count for a lot, and teams have been known to sabotage new hires out of loyalty to former colleagues, competitiveness, or cliquishness. The best way to get teams to be friendly is to have each person pick one thing they can do to welcome the new employee. Then pick someone (or ask for a volunteer) to be the new hire's "buddy" and acclimate them to the team and the organization.

Finally, ensure your calendar is open on their first day. There is nothing worse than starting a new job where your boss is in meetings all day, and you've been relegated to filling out forms in the break room.

BRING THEM INTO THE FOLD

Day 1 Morning: When your new employee shows up, meet them the second they walk through the door. If you're their manager, make sure they come right to you. Many organizations make orientation the very first contact with the organization. They send the employees to a designated training room, away from the people with whom they'll be working, and start the indoctrination. We're fine with starting the orientation in the afternoon, but the morning tends to be a bad idea. [Note: If you're onboarding for a night shift, then just adjust the schedule accordingly].

Have you ever seen nature films where the baby duck hatches and bonds to the first creature it sees, even if it's not a duck? New employees are the same way. They're excited, and a little anxious, and they're going to reach out to, and bond with, the first person who reciprocates. Many organizations say, "we want people bonded to the organization, not individual managers, so that's why orientation comes first." It's a lovely sentiment, but it ignores reality. You can bond people to other people, not to companies. We all know the old adage: You join a company, but quit a manager. And as we've demonstrated throughout this book, it's very true.

If you're the manager of this new employee, here's one more disturbing thought. If your employee starts bonding with other new hires from their orientation class, they may be bonded to people who are working for terrible managers. So your new employee's perspective could be distorted and attempts to bond with them jeopardized. Yes, you can undo this contamination, but why exert all that extra effort if you can avoid the problem in the first place?

When the new hire comes to you first thing, you want to accomplish a few goals. First, act as a representative of the company, and ensure that they have a good image of it. Second, give them a good image of their new colleagues and the company's leadership. This is not the time to vent your frustration and dump on your boss or the CEO. Third, tell them how important and valued their job is and how excited you are to have them in this role. Fourth, in a very positive way, give them the nutshell version of the work they'll be doing. Again, this is not the time or place to be negative or tell them about all the roadblocks they're going to encounter.

Finally, introduce them to their "buddy." What's the buddy (and why do most effective organizations have some sort of buddy system)? The buddy is someone who meets weekly with this person for the first month and then every few weeks for the first six months or so. It is somebody to help guide them through the organization. While the manager would be the easiest and most likely choice, hierarchical power dynamics mean it's better if it's somebody other than the manager. The role of the buddy is best filled by someone who can ask questions like *"How are you holding up?" "Feeling overwhelmed?" "How can I help you be even more effective?" "Do you know where the bathrooms are?"* The buddy makes sure that the new person always has some personal connection.

The buddy system may seem silly, but it's based on psychologically sound ideas. Imagine that you're a new kid in a new high school, and you're looking at all these strange faces in the cafeteria. Wouldn't it be nice if one kid came over and said, "Hey, come over and eat with us?" Admit it; you'd be relieved. That's exactly the feeling we're talking about. In every study we conduct, the cruel politics of high school are not lost when we grow into adulthood and enter the workforce. They still exist. Introduce the new person to as many people as you possibly can, and have those people be as welcoming and excited as possible. Remember that people often leave their old workplaces with a bang (a party and gifts), so you want them to enter their new workplace with equal fanfare.

The buddy can also orient them to all the basic procedures that we sometimes forget about. Things like how/when paychecks arrive, how to use the phones, bathroom locations, and the best local restaurants, etc.

Day 1 Afternoon: As we mentioned earlier, this is a fine time to conduct a formal orientation. If your orientation takes a full day or more, you can continue it the next day. Just make sure you catch up with them before they leave the first day. You only need a few minutes, but you want to check in and see how they're doing. And you must ask the following question: *I know starting a new job can feel overwhelming, but if you ever feel* *overwhelmed or frustrated or even like quitting, will you feel comfortable sharing that with me?*

Asking this question builds a psychological bond and a sense of obligation. So if your new hire ever feels like quitting, they're significantly more likely to come and talk to you.

Week 1: Sometime during their first week, we suggest having a pizza party or ice cream or lunch out or something similar. Remember, they probably had a party when they left their previous job, so it's nice to equal that enthusiasm at their new job. If your entire team is remote, then pay for a delivery service to provide lunch for each of your employees.

Also, if you make new hires fun for your current staff, they're much more likely to actually help new hires integrate and show them the ropes. Why do the more senior fraternity members haze the pledges? Because they were hazed themselves.

Another very successful technique is to have a senior leader stop by and greet the new employee (just make sure the executive knows the new employee's name). It's a thrill for most employees to meet the CEO or someone close (depending on the size of your organization). And nothing says "we really care about you and we're excited to have you here" more than when a busy executive makes the time to stop by and say "hi."

Finally, encourage your employees to complete their one welcome task. It's important to create a sense of family. For a few weeks, the new person is going to feel like an outsider, but it's crucial to minimize this stage and get them integrated as quickly as possible. Otherwise, you risk losing them, literally and figuratively, to their former culture and coworkers. So the best thing to do is to check in with them every single day.

Month 1 – 3: Changing jobs is stressful for most people. It is a time of upheaval and great change. It is also a chance for growth and development. During this fragile period, you, as the leader, have a chance to forge a relationship that will endure. You can build a bond that will last you years. This bonding primarily takes place in the first month. Once you've established your relationship and helped to build networks with peers or colleagues, you can then move into the first performance review.

The first performance review should be done right after the one-month mark, not 90 days as is typical. The purpose of this first review is to give them guidance and let them know how they're doing. Then, you want to find out how they are feeling, and what this experience has been like for them. This is not a formal evaluation, but informal coaching and checking in. Let them know that your philosophy is to coach them to success. You want this person to succeed, so make sure that you're giving them the feedback they need to succeed. Waiting 90 days to do all of this is way too long, and most 90-day reviews are designed to evaluate probationary periods, not guide and coach.

In this coaching session, you should focus on three things:

1. Positive Reinforcement – Give your new hire positive feedback. First, they made it through the roughest part of being a new hire. Also, pick out some specific job-related tasks that they did well. Give them some positive guidance too.
2. Describe Their Experience – Ask the employee to talk about what the first month has been like for them: the good, the bad, and the ideas for improvement. Maybe they could compare it to their experience as a new employee at their former job as well.
3. Clarify Expectations – Discuss their job role, make sure they understand the expectations regarding their performance, who they work with, and what they are responsible for.

After you've gone through these three items, you can then get them cycled into your Shoves and Tugs conversations.

PUTTING IT TOGETHER

Is Roger going to stay or bolt? Luckily, you remembered to have the employee handbook sent to him ahead of time so that he could read up on the company. Then you sent a card signed by all the staff and a roster of the entire team so that he would get to know all of his coworkers. Last week you met with your sales staff and discussed Roger coming on board and got them really psyched up for his arrival. You know that Roger will be welcomed into the fold. You shake his hand as he comes into your office, and you tell him how excited you are to have him on board.

You talk to him a little bit about this job role and give him a brief rundown of what his first day will look like: Breakfast with you, an introduction to Carl- who will be his peer mentor, and then a tour of the sales department. Then off to lunch with the sales staff, an orientation with Ginny from HR, then back to your office for a short check-in before he goes home. It sounds like a busy day, but Roger looks eager and happy. You've set everything in motion for a good welcome, and you have a solid plan for the new few months.

The statistics are on your side. You feel confident that Roger will stay.

DEADLY SIN #6
Letting Them Leave

IMAGINE THAT YOU'RE THE PRESIDENT of a mid-sized printing company. You're in the middle of placing a supply order when your Sales Director rushes through the door and tells you that Self-Pub just called and said they will no longer need your services. Self-Pub is one of your biggest clients, and they've accounted for one-third of your revenue for the past five years. What do you do? Do you just let them go? Or do you immediately jump on the phone and work to get them back?

Now imagine that you own a home remodeling company. You're in the middle of a very large and labor-intensive renovation. Jake, one of your best carpenters, solemnly approaches you at the end of the day on Friday to give you his two-weeks' notice. What do you do? What do you say?

If you believe that the adage "If you love somebody set them free" applies here, then you're putting yourself in a losing position. Most people are unwilling to accept a goodbye from a major client; they call them, make personal visits, send gifts, and log countless hours of wooing. Yet these same people often just roll over and play dead when an employee, even a stellar one, says that they want to leave. Why is that? What is so different about these two scenarios that cause people to respond so disparately?

In the following pages, you are going to see why it is so important to drop the whole "set them free" attitude and adopt a new saying: "Don't give up without a fight." In the next section, we'll spell out a 3-step process that will have you fighting and winning the battle to keep your employees when they tell you that they want to quit.

SLOW THEM DOWN

Quick and painless, that's what they want, like pulling a bandage off a skinned knee. Employees generally hate giving their boss any bad news, especially if they like their boss. And telling your boss that you want to quit counts as giving bad news. So they want to give the news FAST. They want to be in and out of the office and have it over and done with.

Imagine you're the manager of a very high-profile advertising project. Your skills are invaluable to the success of your team and this assignment. You've already worked with this client for over a year, the project will continue for another year, and you know all the ins-and-outs of their product line. You generally like your job and take pride in what you do. You get along very well with your boss and feel like she has been a mentor to you. But you have another job offer, with a big promotion, and they want you to start next month. You need to tell your boss that you want to accept this new job offer. How do you feel? How do you feel with each successive day that goes by?

Leadership IQ polled 217 employees who quit their job within the last year. When asked about their emotional state, 87% of the employees said they felt very anxious about telling their boss that they planned on leaving. And with each day that passed without telling, they got more and more nervous. Through further interviews, we discovered that not only did they want to feel relief from this growing nervousness, but they also wanted to "get it over with" so that they "wouldn't change their mind."

Quitting can be a monumental decision, and employees can feel deeply conflicted and unsure about their decision to quit. They don't want their decision challenged because they know that they could be talked out of it. Employees also feel anxious about telling their boss. They're desperately hoping that they can tell their boss quickly, with no real conversation, and get out of the office as fast as possible.

When employees enter your office to tell you that they're quitting, they're unsure, anxious, emotionally fragile, and easily swayed. They want to deliver their message as quickly as possible so they can feel emotional relief and avoid getting talked out of their decision.

The question for leaders becomes: "How do you slow this process down so you give the employee a chance to reconsider?" You don't want the employee to make a rash decision that they could end up regretting. And stories abound of employees rashly quitting one company only to find they're more miserable at their new employer. Your first job is to slow them down, and that process has three stages.

STEP 1: WITHHOLD RELIEF
Stop, Look, Listen, and Question. Stop what you are doing. Find a quiet space to talk, either in your office or a meeting room. Tell them that you want to hear more about what they just told you and do it immediately. Look at their body language. How comfortable or uncomfortable do they seem? The more uncomfortable they are, the greater the likelihood you can convince them to stay. Listen to their story. Ask to hear the whole saga. Stay neutral and listen with an open mind. Gather all the data, both flattering and unflattering, about your company and about you. Ask questions. Find out all the reasons they want to

leave your company. Find out what the new position will offer them. Gather as much data as possible.

Quiet Down, Speak Up. Ask your employee to keep quiet about their potential decision for now. Get your employee to agree to keep it under wraps until you have fully fleshed out the details together. Why? Because if they don't tell people, then it isn't set in stone. What reason do you give to your employee? Let them know that you don't want them to limit their options at this point. At the same time, you need to speak to the people above you about the potential loss of this employee. It's important to tell your boss about it within an hour of your meeting with the employee. Bring the data you gathered in your listening session and brainstorm about what you might be able to do or offer to keep your employee.

24-Hour Waiting Period. At the end of your listening session with the employee, ask them to hold off on their final decision until you've had a chance to present them with all the options. Give a 24-hour waiting period and set up a meeting for the next day. This will give you time to talk with your bosses and see what, if any, options you can offer to keep your employee.

End with Kudos. If you end your meeting on a positive note, it will be fresh on the employee's mind. Let your employee know that you appreciate their candor and that they are truly a valued member of your team, and that's why you want to take some time to figure out how you can keep them. The employee will likely see your efforts as a sign of their value and may genuinely think twice about their reasons for leaving.

STEP 2: MAKE YOUR OFFER

It's important to set up a meeting for as early as possible the day after your employee makes their announcement. The meeting should consist of the employee, you, and someone higher up and representing the organization. It's important to have a higher-up there (or

Board member if you're the CEO trying to retain an executive) to demonstrate your seriousness.

Before the meeting, you want to spend some time creating valid arguments that show how staying with your company is in the employee's best interest. Now, if you are thoroughly convinced that there is no valid argument, then you've lost them because you won't be able to sell this convincingly (and it's just not a good way to operate). But if you are convinced there is a valid argument, then you might be able to address the concerns they expressed in the previous meeting. Maybe it involves working for another manager, moving to a new department, or creating a new job. Whatever the issue is, you've got to figure out what you're going to do.

When you begin your meeting, start by stating all the concerns that they presented to you. You want to validate those concerns, but you also need to address the "grass is greener" issue about the new company by exposing it as unrealistic. Walk through what it's really going to be like over at that other company. You don't want to do it in a nasty, blaming way, but you do want to challenge their arguments that it's beautiful over there and terrible over here. Also, have your higher-up point out the benefits of staying with your organization and the benefits to the employee's career and future.

Most importantly, you want to make sure that you solve the employee's problem. The pitch is all well and good, but, ultimately, you've actually got to do something to solve the employee's problems. This employee has decided to quit working for you, and this is a potential high performer, so they've probably got a valid reason for wanting to leave. It's important to come to the table with a few options for fixing the issues that the employee has presented.

Once you have presented your offer, and made it as enticing as possible, you can ask your employee for a final decision. Hopefully, your employee is feeling comfortable, valued, and esteemed by the end of this meeting – all of which makes a YES response more likely. However, sometimes roadblocks still exist: A spouse or partner who is leaning in the other direction, or an aggressive organization heavily recruiting your employee.

STEP 3: CONFRONT ROADBLOCKS

Spouses and partners can have agendas of their own. The best way to deal with them is by speaking to them directly. Many times an employee will say something like, "Well, I'm really considering staying, but my wife is sold on the idea of this new job with CeeCorp." The best way for a manager to respond is to say something like, "Maybe I can talk to her and try to understand why she likes CeeCorp so much and let her know what we have to offer here." In order to keep the best employees, sometimes managers need to sell significant others on the idea of staying as much as they need to sell employees on staying. If this is the case, then you need to spend some time talking to this person, addressing their concerns, and making your offer clear to them as well.

As far as the competing organization goes, you've got to eliminate them. If they have attempted to steal away your best people before, you can bet they will try to do it again. When your employee makes the decision to stay with you, the next step is to give the employee a very formal script to use for declining the offer with this other organization. Ideally, you should be in the room while they're making the call. However, you should do what feels best for the employee. Oftentimes, employees will feel comfortable making the call with you present. It's moral support for them.

The script should be something along the lines of, "CeeCorp, I know this will be a disappointment to you, but I won't be accepting your offer. I'm going to stay here at ABusiness. After talking with several senior executives, it's clear to me I made a mistake in thinking about leaving. This has nothing to do with money or counteroffers; this is just about what's best for me and my career. My decision is final."

The goal of this call is two-fold. First, you want to shut down the competitor and make sure they don't think about coming back and poaching your employees. Second, you want to make the employee's decision final, psychologically and verbally.

In sum, it is important to fight for your employees. Organizations that take the time to listen to employees that want to leave, and genuinely attempt to fix things in order to keep them, retain up to 50% more employees than organizations that just let them leave.

PUTTING IT TOGETHER

Let's return to our opening example with Jake, our carpenter who wants to quit. Jake solemnly approaches you at the end of the day on Friday to give you his two-weeks notice. What do you do?

Imagine it goes like this. Jake approaches, gives his speech, and you say, "Wow, Jake, I must say, this is quite a surprise. I really want to talk this through with you. Give me five minutes, and we'll meet in the trailer to talk about it."

Five minutes later, you sit down in the trailer with him and say, "I really want to know about what led to this decision so that I can understand it fully."

Jake responds, "Well, a few weeks ago, the Construction Supervisor at Urbana General Contracting called me and said he had seen my work at the Historic Home Show. He said they really liked my work and wanted me to come on board and design cabinetry for their retail construction division."

To which you reply, "Hmmmm. I didn't realize you were interested in focusing on cabinetry."

And Jake says, "Well, I don't want to just do cabinetry, but they offered me a really good salary."

You think it over and say, "Must be good. Can I ask what they offered?"

And Jake says, "$5 an hour more than I am making now."

You nod in agreement and ask, "There must have been some other things about the job that interested you."

Jake replies, "I really like creating the designs, I think it will be pretty interesting."

You say, "You have a great eye, I can see why that job would grab you. I guess you don't feel like you get to do much of that here."

He says, "Not really. I definitely get to do a variety of carpentry here, which is cool, but I'm usually not the one designing it.

You respond, "Were there other things you wanted to do here but couldn't?"

"Not really. I mean, I really like working for you, and the guys here are great. It's really a lot of fun. It's mostly that Urbana is a big company, and I think I can make more money there and probably get a promotion."

And the talk goes on for a while. Finally, you say, "Jake, I think you are a really great carpenter, and I really like working with you. That is why I really want to take some time and think about what you just told me. I don't know whether or not we can work something out, but I don't want you to limit your options right now. So I'm asking you to consider keeping this quiet until Monday. Then let's meet at my office at 9:00 a.m., and we can discuss it some more."

Jake agrees and you, as the owner and president of the company, have some hard thinking to do. You call up your site Foreman and run some ideas past him. You agree to bring him in for the next meeting too.

You all sit down in your office for the Monday morning meeting, and you say, "Jake, I've had a rough weekend. I've really thought about everything you've told me. I think you are a fantastic carpenter, as does the Foreman, and we really hope you will choose to stay here. Although we are a small company, I think we have some great opportunities for you. The great thing about working here is the variety of projects and the family attitude. We'd like to offer you more choices about which projects you take. We think you are very talented and very versatile and would be glad to have you on the projects of your choosing. At Urbana, you'd really be doing the same type of designs and projects all the time, which might get boring for a creative person like you. Second, you do have a very good eye. We'd like to really see what you can do and start you off on designing. I think the rest of the crew would really be behind that; they respect you and the work you've done. I think another great thing about working here is that we all really work together well. I'm not sure you'll find that at a big place like Urbana, where most of the laborers are per diem and come and go. I know they've offered you some good weekly money. I can't really do that. But what I can offer you is a bonus after each project that we finish…"

Jake feels good about his potential at the company and decides to stay. With your coaching, he is able to tell Urbana that he is not accepting their offer. He also calls home to tell his wife, who is happy that he is staying with your company because she knows everyone there and feels like Jake is really well-respected. You were successful. How did you do it? You slowed him down, made your offer, and confronted any roadblocks that prevented you from keeping your best carpenter.

DEADLY SIN #7
Turning Your Back

CATHY WAS A GREAT SOCIAL Worker. Her clients respected her, the staff looked up to her, she did more than her share of work, and she was a very pleasant person. But despite everything you did to try to keep her, she really wanted to go into private practice. How do you feel towards Cathy? What do you do now?

Maybe you feel a bit angry or betrayed. After all, you mentored her all these years, thinking that she'd take over your department after you got promoted to Director. Maybe you feel silly, like you should have left to go into private practice as well. Sure, the temptation is just to break ties with her and be done with it. Or decide that she wasn't as great as you thought and bad-mouth her after she leaves. Is that the best direction to take this? Probably not, because while it makes us feel better in the short term, it cuts off our opportunities in the long run.

BOOMERANGS, CLIENTS, AND LIAISONS

When people leave their company on good terms, they tend to keep that company on their mind. They see it as either a good place to work, a good place to patronize, or a good place to refer to others. When people leave remembering that they generally liked working for your company, they are more likely to return in the future. We call these people *boomerangs*. Boomerangs may come back to you at some point in the future.

There are three good reasons to like boomerangs. One, they're up to speed, which makes them quicker to train when they come back. So somebody who quits you, and two years later comes back, is up to speed much faster than a typical new employee. Two, they already understand your values and culture. And three, they often bring back innovative new ideas to keep you from getting stale.

Next, former employees can become future clients. Depending on your industry, they can bring lots of business your way. This is the result of former employees seeing your company as a good place to refer to others. Sometimes former employees can be a great source of referrals for potential employees or customers. For example, at Leadership IQ, we have research assistants. Recently, one of our fabulous research assistants left us to go to graduate school. While we were saddened by the loss, we were thrilled that she sent two of her classmates from college to interview for her former position.

KEEP IT POSITIVE

How do you make the goodbye a "good goodbye" and leave the road open to future relationships? The key is to keep things positive. What we found is that there is a very simple way to end the working relationship while maintaining the connection:

1. Throw a Party

2. Touch Base
3. Update

Throwing a goodbye party may sound trite and overly simplistic. But what happens when you throw a party for a valued employee who is leaving? You let them know that they were important and will be missed. It also lets them formally say goodbye to all of their colleagues. The key is to keep the party simple. Another positive result of the party is that it lets the employee leave feeling connected to their coworkers and cements the homey atmosphere of your corporation.

Sometimes when employees leave and then start at another company, they are shocked at the lack of fanfare that greets them at the new workplace. They go from knowing everyone and feeling comfortable, to knowing no one and feeling lonely. This lack of fanfare contrasted with the goodbye party can sometimes shock employees into boomeranging back to you fairly quickly.

Second, it is important to give your former employee a call or an email to touch base 30 to 60 days after they leave. The goal is to "touch base" and see how they are doing in their new job. This keeps the connection going by placing you on their minds at a time when they have so much new information to remember. Finally, you should provide occasional updates about job openings, new programs, etc. You never know when you can get them to boomerang back or refer someone to you.

GATHER DATA

Whenever an employee leaves, it is important to find out their final reasons for ending the working relationship and their feelings about your organization. While it's easy to simply say goodbye and cut ties, it is more beneficial to you and your organization to have a formal exit interview to gather data. The reasons for the exit interview are twofold. First, you need to figure out what, if anything, could be fixed to lure this employee back. Second, you need to diagnose and fix any problems that could push other employees away and lead them to quit.

The exercise of conducting the exit interview does little, in and of itself, to bring employees back. It is the data gathered during the interview that is of use. Unfortunately, many companies don't look at or use the information gathered in these sessions. When Leadership IQ polled companies about their use of exit interviews, approximately 95% said they conduct them, but only 42% said they actually do anything based on the results. Many of them said that they weren't sure what questions they needed to ask and also that they didn't know who should get the results.

First and foremost, exit interviews should be done after the employee has formally left his or her position, and second, the interview should be conducted by someone besides the employee's former manager. After an employee is a bit settled into their new job, they are less likely to feel coerced and more likely to give honest feedback. At that point, they have no formal ties to your organization and, thus, nothing to lose.

Ideally, an outside consultant or an HR professional, or somebody from an entirely separate part of the organization should conduct the interview. A study by two researchers, Joseph Zarandona and Michael Camuso, compared exit interviews done internally versus exit interviews done externally. What they found was that when employees were interviewed by their manager, 38% said they left for money reasons, but when they were asked by a third party outside researcher, only 12% said money was the issue. When they were asked by managers whether poor supervision was an issue, only 4% said yes. When they were asked the same question by a third party, 24% agreed that poor supervision was the issue. This study highlights the importance of having an interviewer with as many degrees of separation from the employee as possible. If you want accurate and honest information, you need a neutral third party.

It is important to ask the old standby questions: "What made you leave? Did you share this with your manager? What did you like most? What did you like least? Would you consider returning to the organization?" And it is even more important to ask a follow-up question to each of the responses that an employee gives. Interviewers need to be skilled data gatherers who take the job seriously and know that the goal is to uncover the *real* reasons employees leave an organization. They need to know that their goal is to find the problems so that others can fix them. Interviewers need to be thorough.

Finally, where should the exit interview data go? The answer is, to everyone who manages or leads people in the organization. Every manager should know why their employees left, and every leader, including the CEO, should look at the overall results to see if there are problems endemic to the organization or particular departments.

Will the "Quitting Virus" Spread?

One of the most common questions we get about employees who quit is whether they'll make all your other employees want to quit. Here's our answer: One of the biggest reasons for conducting Shoves and Tugs conversations at least every quarter, and preferably every month, is that you'll already know if any other employees are thinking about quitting. The only way for you to find out is to ask, and if you follow the script we gave you previously, you'll be in great shape. Additionally, if you conduct regular Shoves and Tugs conversations, you can ask your employees what they're thinking without looking panicked that someone just quit. This will just be part of your normal monthly Shoves and Tugs conversation.

If the employee that quit is assuming a managerial role and you're worried that they'll try to steal away your best employees, here's a great technique: Mentor them. If this is their first management job, tell them how excited you are that they have this opportunity to create a brand-new team without having to tackle the emotional baggage that comes from managing former peers. This will make them seriously reconsider taking anyone.

Then, regardless of their previous management experience, ask how you can help them. Be there for them. Serve as a mentor. You want to do this for two reasons: First, you'll make them feel guilty if they consider stealing your people away (and it's often just enough to dissuade them). Second, do you know the old saying, "Keep your friends close and your enemies closer?" Well, the more you keep in contact with them, the more likely you are to glean some insight into their next steps. That may be just the competitive intelligence you need to stay one step ahead.

The bottom line is that regardless of how betrayed you feel and how much you want revenge, you can't really do anything to punish quitting employees. And if you try to do something retaliatory, you'll only make yourself look petty and mean-spirited. We've all had the occasional revenge fantasy, but the smartest move after someone quits is to keep your cool, keep as close to the quitting employee as possible, and keep as close to your remaining employees as possible.

And remember, "dissing" the departed employee to your remaining employees is unlikely to guilt them into staying (that's not how guilt works). Instead, what will happen is that when they do feel like quitting, they'll be too scared to tell you.

PUTTING IT TOGETHER

Cathy was a great Social Worker. While you feel bad about her leaving, you want to keep the relationship with her going. On her last day of work, you and your staff throw her a lovely goodbye luncheon in the staff lounge. Everyone has pitched in to make homemade treats, and at the end of the party, you present her with a personalized clipboard as a goodbye gift from you and the staff. Cathy says a tearful farewell and promises to keep in touch.

Two weeks later, an associate from Human Resources had an exit interview with Cathy. He discovers that, while Cathy had planned on eventually going into private practice, she had some conflicts with one of her colleagues that hastened her departure. Still, Cathy left feeling positive about her work at your agency and her relationship with you. One month down the road, you pick up the phone to give Cathy a call and see how she is doing. She is not available, but you leave her a nice voicemail message letting her know that you are thinking of her and hoping that her practice is taking off. Later that day, you see that she sent you an email saying that she was pleasantly surprised by your message and that she hopes to reach you soon because she wants to refer a client to your agency.

Who knows what will happen further down the road? Maybe Cathy will return to work for you someday. Or maybe she will simply send more clients your way. But, whatever happens, the relationship is there because you didn't turn your back.

CONCLUSION

Imagine you're the CEO of a large hospital. You're facing staffing shortages in your most important roles, your overall turnover number is horrible, the board is breathing down your neck, a nurses union is trying to organize your hospital, and if you don't act fast, you could lose your job.

Imagine you're the Assistant Manager for a large discount store. You've got 80 direct reports, they all make minimum wage (or slightly over), turnover exceeds 100%, you've got lots of seasonal workers, and you can't name more than 30 of your employees.

DON'T TRY TO SAVE THE WORLD

The Core is a highly entertaining disaster film released in 2003 (we're leadership experts, not film critics, so take our review with a grain of salt). In the film, the Earth's core stops rotating and our planet's magnetic sheath collapses, meaning the planet is about to be destroyed. So a manned mission is dispatched to the center of the Earth to "jumpstart" the planet. Among the heroes dispatched to save the Earth are Dr. Josh Keyes (an Indiana Jones-like geophysicist who ultimately saves the planet) and his best friend, Dr. Serge Leveque (a French atomic weapons expert, husband, and father of 2 little girls).

After the death of their first crew member, Dr. Keyes becomes overwhelmed by the prospect of trying to save everyone on the planet from certain death. To Serge, he says, "My God, the whole thing just feels so overwhelming. Do we really have a chance?" Serge knowingly pats his friend on the shoulder and says, "Josh, my friend, nobody can save the world. It's just too much. You are trying to save 6 billion lives. I am just trying to save 3 lives; my wife and daughters. That's all I can comprehend. That's all I can do. But I can do that."

Here's our advice to executives and managers: Don't try to save 6 billion people, just try to save three. If you try to save the world, your brain will overload. It's just too much. Just find a few people you can save and put your energy there.

There's a dirty little secret about large-scale retention initiatives: They oversell and underdeliver. Millions of dollars get spent, and the results are underwhelming. Every so often, an organization will claim success from a large-scale initiative, but you'll usually find that the whole organization didn't improve; just a few managers did. And that's the point.

To improve retention, you've got to act locally, at the individual level. Even if you're the CEO of a Fortune 100 company, improving retention is a local initiative. Let's imagine you're the CEO of an organization with 10,000 employees. With a typical 10:1 span of control, you've probably got 1,000 leaders. And let's say that around 40% of the workforce is a top priority for your retention efforts (i.e., 4,000 employees are high performers and/or in hard-to-replace roles). So 1,000 managers have to focus on retaining 4,000 employees. For people that hate to do math in their heads, every manager has to retain 4 people.

Would you like to retain 80% of the workforce? Of course. But as we discussed earlier, you've got to start with the critical people and positions.

When we tell executives that they need to retain their most critical 4,000 employees, they get a bit panicky. As you might expect, the initial reaction is to create a major initiative to transform retention practices. But when we tell them that every manager has to retain their 4 most critical people, the task doesn't seem so daunting.

"Many hands make light work," goes the saying. And nowhere is that more true than in retention efforts.

First Steps

For senior executives, the first step is simple: Train every manager on how to retain a few of their most critical people. Most leaders commit at least a few of the deadly sins outlined in this book, so give every leader a day of training on how to implement the practices in this book. (At the very least, make every manager read this book.) Before you spend millions of dollars on major initiatives, invest in a day of training and some books. It's much less expensive and exponentially more effective.

For managers, your first steps are essentially to implement the skills from this book. And if you start with the tactics below, you'll be off to a great start. You'll start to see your employee retention improve, and then you can get to work on everything else.

1. Create a retention Priority Grid for your direct reports.
2. Conduct Shoves and Tugs conversations with each of your top retention priorities (while listening deeply).
3. Work on fixing at least one Shove you discovered during those conversations.
4. Change the initiation process for new hires. Send a welcome card to every new hire's home before they start, find some volunteers for a buddy system and meet with your

new hires before they begin their orientation.
5. Analyze your Shoves and Tugs conversations, as well as your exit interview data, and find one opportunity for self-improvement.

A Final Thought

This book was designed to be easy to read and implement. There are a few key mistakes that virtually every leader in every organization makes, and these mistakes (aka deadly sins) undermine employee retention efforts. But if you take the necessary steps to correct and eliminate the deadly sins, you'll leapfrog your competition.

We've seen organizations correct the deadly sins in under 30 days and radically transform their ability to retain employees. Correcting the deadly sins doesn't require a major initiative involving large budgets and an army of consultants. Correcting the deadly sins requires an understanding of the problem and the disciplined execution of the solution.

CPSIA information can be obtained
at www.ICGtesting.com
Printed in the USA
LVHW021155200423
744760LV00001B/55